MILES TO THE TOP

From Survival to Significance

LINDA MILES

Miles to the Top: From Survival to Significance
By Linda Miles

Crescendo Publishing, LLC
300 Carlsbad Village Drive
Ste. 108A, #443
Carlsbad, California 92008-2999
GetPublished@CrescendoPublishing.com
1-877-575-8814

ISBN: 978-1-944177-94-2 (p)
ISBN: 978-1-944177-95-9 (e)

Cover photo credit: Michael Barton from Princeton, WV

Printed in the United States of America
10 9 8 7 6 5 4 3 2 1

Message from the Author

https://www.youtube.com/watch?v=aquPuyOu7O4

Do you believe the AMERICAN DREAM is alive and well? It IS, but **ONLY** for those who have the right spirit of *whatever comes my way, I promise to learn from it then spread that spirit and knowledge to the masses...*

We never know when one choice in our life will change our direction and cause disappointment. That same disappointment will often lead us on a different—but fabulous—new path. That happened to me when I decided *not* to go to work for the FBI in DC like so many of my recruited classmates from the high school in our small West Virginia town. Then, another disappointment came several months after I made my DC decision. Even though I had graduated at seventeen, the bank I applied to work for would not hire me until I turned eighteen, which was a whole summer away.

I thought I was out of luck and out of work options until my Sunday school teacher, Mr. Jameson, told my mom that an Army Reservist friend of his in Bluefield—a dentist by the name of Dr. Jim Nelson—needed a receptionist. This kind-hearted dentist knew I was planning to marry my high school sweetheart when he came home on leave after basic training with the Air Force, and he was okay with me being short term. That stroke of luck was the start of a fifty-five-year career of a lifetime. Little did I know that my starting salary of $125 per month would lead me to starting two very successful companies that became a beacon of light for hundreds of others to start their similar businesses.

The success of my consulting clients, audiences, and those I have mentored truly was the essence of my own success over those years. I believe what you put into the universe comes back in spades. I did not do it alone. My corporate team and husband ran the office while I traveled extensively. Both of my children worked at the office for about six years. I learned the spirit of abundance—giving back—from my mom. Mom was my hero. Dad gave me the entrepreneurial gene.

This book, a flashback to my formative years as a child, teen, young military wife and mom, entrepreneur, and volunteer allows the reader to know that opportunities are everywhere. Going after those opportunities means seeing a need that is not being addressed, learning the skills to conquer the weaknesses in that profession or business, perfecting your own skills, then sharing those skills with the dozens to thousands of others you may come in contact with during your business life.

I remember my mom saying to me after I had been in business about twenty years, "Bobbie [my youngest sister] says she doesn't understand it! Linda's out there traveling all over the country and world. She stays in fine hotels, speaks, consults, and writes books. We had the same parents, same schools, and such, but here I am—still a secretary for a school principal in Lynchburg, Virginia making $13 per hour, and Linda is the owner of a very successful company." I immediately called Bobbie and said, "You were the youngest and the smartest child in our family of four. You could do exactly what I'm doing, but it takes lots of hard work and time [in business, we are all overnight successes in only 15 years!]. All you have to do is find something you love doing. Learn how to do it really well, then teach other people how to learn to love it too." My sister's response was, "I'd be arrested!"

The truth of the matter is, not everyone is cut out to be an entrepreneur. The first few years are very lean, and there are no owner paychecks. You should have a back-up support team with earning power. The first few years, you'll truly *want* to give up! Many folks give up right before the magic starts. Thankfully, I did not give up— even though my early team members said they knew I was going to make it when I stopped looking at daily Dental Help Wanted Ads in the local newspaper (hoping to find a dentist so I could go back to my comfort zone of a steady income). My advice is to **NEVER GIVE UP.**

In the 50s and 60s, higher education was not a "must" as it is today. My advice to all younger folks? Get your degree. While it doesn't guarantee a job, it certainly increases one's chances for a stronger possibility.

My second piece of advice is that if you have entrepreneurial yearnings, discover *what* you enjoy most.

Learn how to do it very well, and start your own business after thirty-five, when you have earned and saved enough to leave your full-time job. I can't imagine staying in a job or business that you dislike. Thinking out of the box and getting out of the box to follow one's dream is the most frightening yet exciting thing you will ever experience.

Next on my list is to learn to control costs and *save!*

You will need a rainy day fund with six months of living and operating costs set aside for emergencies. And, you'll need a fully funded retirement portfolio by the time you turn fifty-five to sixty. How sad to see those who have no money-management skills spend more each year than they earn. Eventually—with poor credit, no earning power due to illness, accidents, or loss of job/business— these "pretend-to-have-it-all" folks become destitute.

Even in our Air Force days, the first twenty-one years of our marriage, we learned to save for the rainy day. Having felt the stress of almost being destitute with lost Air Force pay records in California, we never wanted to experience that again. We budgeted wisely as newlyweds and young parents. We always lived below our means, or certainly within them. We didn't eat out, as eating at home was in vogue. The other reason was there were not many places to eat out in the 60s. Every payday while in Mobile, Alabama, our twice per month date night treat was going with LaDona to Colonial Dixie's—a drive-in with hamburgers. After our two children were born, we took them everywhere with us since we could not afford sitters. We did not smoke, drink, or have extensive wardrobes. There were no "high maintenance costs" back then either for beauty salons, nail salons, massage studios, or gyms.

As our early years' income grew, we saved for emergencies like buying new tires or car/appliance maintenance. Credit cards were not around much back in those days, so what we had, we paid for or we did without. Vacations were often "stay-cations" by finding something local to enjoy like public beaches near Mobile and Miami. It amazes me how many young families today don't keep logs of *where* their money goes. Many would be shocked with their $300 per month Starbucks habit or their $500-$700 per month eating out budgets. Imagine where they would be in twenty years saving that $1000 per month! Without a where-its-going log, you can never know what is unnecessary. Seeing your money *make* money each year is actually fun entertainment, knowing it will allow you to live life to the fullest in retirement. That statement "A fool and his money are soon parted" is so true.

My goal for this book is to enlighten those who feel they can't become successful due to their meager beginnings. Or for those who are embarking on a career path that is *not* what they truly like. I'd like to challenge them and give them the courage to jump out of the box in which they feel they are being trapped. It is also for the ultra-successful, who can identify with the lessons learned along my life path. I encourage each of you to write your life story. We all have a unique and interesting life story in many ways. Some have had less than ideal circumstances to overcome, but their life story is even more important to share. Start sharing it now.

All the best,

Linda Miles

Endorsements

Linda Miles is a serious motivator of minds, and she calls for action to better one's self. At our Australian seminars, she always has a "full house." Year after year, dentists and auxiliary staff vote her number one.

Ruth Port, Power2B
Sydney, Australia

Linda Miles understands how to have a life filled with success and framed with significance. Her life story is inspiring, enlightening, and challenging. You'll love this book.

Dr. Nido R. Qubein, President
High Point University

Linda Miles is a shining example of success in business and life. With her reputation of common sense and hard work, Linda built a nationally-recognized practice management consulting business and is known in the dental world as an expert in the field. Linda Miles is a gifted communicator who has lectured to millions of dental auxiliaries and dentists worldwide. Having known Linda for over twenty years, I can confidently say that her greatest gift is her heart for people. From waitresses to CEOs, all are important to her. Linda has a unique ability to tune in to people and encourage them to take bold steps in finding fulfilling life work, and I would not be where I am today without her mentoring and encouragement.

Dianne Watterson, RDH, MBA
Speaker, Author, Consultant

Generosity = Linda Miles.
A woman whose inspiration has changed so many lives across the dental world. Her knack for reading people and truly caring is unique. We all love you, Linda, and know this book is a footprint of your life that you entrusted in all of us to foster.

Kathy Metaxas, Founder/CEO
Platinum Professional Development, Perth, Western Australia

Linda Miles is the most influential Practice Management Consultant of all time. She inspires everyone around her and continually focuses on the positive. She has personally impacted my life and career more than anyone. This book is a must-read for all business owners and entrepreneurs alike.

Tanya A. Brown, DMD, FAGD

It was thirty-one years ago when I was first introduced to Linda Miles. It was not a structured "meet and greet." I was invited to be a "vendor" at a local dental study club. I was the only dental CPA in attendance. I asked the sponsor of the event if I could sit in the conference and listen to the guest speaker, Linda Miles. The conference leader responded, "Of course!" As I was sitting there listening, I said to myself, *Wow... this person really has it all together. Everything she is chatting about makes sense, and is practical.* I even thought, *Every dentist in Maryland needs to hear her! Her lecture was spot on!* Well, in those days, we didn't have iPads to take notes. As a recall, after a day's lecture, I must have had twenty plus pages of "legal paper" notes!

Those who are in the business of Dental Practice Management Consulting need to thank Linda Miles. Linda paved the way for those who have followed by creating a profession within a profession! In my professional opinion, Linda Miles is by far the most influential Dental Practice Management Consultant of our lifetime. Linda is simply the best!

Linda has an abundance of energy that immediately gravitates to those she touches. Linda always has time for a question. And, more importantly, her responses to those questions are filled with thought, creativity, and unselfish inspiration. Linda continues to inspire me through her generous mentorship, guidance, and professional advice!

Linda's new book is a must-read for all business owners and entrepreneurs alike, especially those in the dental profession.

Continued success to all who Linda has touched!

Allen M. Schiff, Dental CPA
President of the Academy of Dental CPAs

Table of Contents

Dedication

For the past twenty-five years, my high school friend Reta Phillips Hill has been telling me to write a book on my life. My question was always, "Who would buy my life story?" Reta said, "Everyone who realizes that you can be successful even with a high school diploma, a lot of hard work, dedication, and a positive attitude." She even shared with me that once, during a difficult time in her life, my audio cassette on the value of change helped her make some changes in her life. But, as busy as I was over the past twenty-five years, concentrating on my life book was not an option. Besides, until we enter into the "winter" phase of our lives, we have not gone full circle.

Reta is one of those lifelong friends who is relentless (in a good way), and she never stopped asking me "When are you writing the book?" So, my friend, I thank you for never giving up on me—and for knowing that after I retired, I'd finally find time to write "the book."

Foreword

Over the course of my career, I have been blessed to have a number of friends and mentors who have helped me along the way. I would not be where I am today if some had not seen in me things I didn't see in myself. I owe a great many people, but one stands head and shoulders above the rest, and that is Linda Miles. Linda personifies the words, "friend," "mentor," "integrity," "perseverance," and "hard work." There are countless people who have "rags to riches" stories. Many struggle to remain humble or kind, and to share their time, wisdom, and wealth with others once they have achieved great success. I have never met a person, male or female, as exceptional as Linda—and I'm quite confident I never will. She's truly "one of a kind!"

My journey with Linda began thirty years ago, when I was an inexperienced dental business team member. I had the good fortune to attend one of her courses, and I felt a bond with her instantly. Her philosophy was so practical, her ideas so common sense, and she was so gracious in spending time with me during her programs I attended that I knew I wanted to be just like her! My doctor's office (Dr. John Steinberg, where I was employed as a dental business assistant) flourished as I applied her systems and principles. After experiencing that success, I decided I wanted to work with her. I approached her and shared my dream, and she shared with me the credentials and experience I would need in order to be considered as a member of her consulting team. After about two years of attending all her courses, starting my own consulting business, becoming a "fledging" speaker, communicating with her regularly, and downright badgering her relentlessly, she hired me! The rest, as they say, is history!

This book is a must-read for anyone who wants to find the courage to take risks, who struggles with confidence, who has humble beginnings—but who has passion and a great work ethic, regardless of their chosen profession. While Linda's experience and success have come through the profession of dentistry, the lessons she's learned and is sharing transcend all professions and can be applied to anyone seeking to achieve both personal and professional success. Countless thousands of dental professionals have benefitted from Linda's expertise, and now people outside the profession of dentistry can benefit from her experiences through this book. The lessons she is sharing are invaluable.

While Linda has officially retired from the speaking and consulting business, she still continues to be a guest speaker for philanthropic causes, sharing her message of hope, inspiration, and a value-based life. She continues to give back to her friends, family, her profession, and those suffering hardships. Most recently, she participated in the Lucy Hobbs Project for Benco Dental, a project dedicated to helping women be successful in dentistry. Linda is also the co-founder of Oral Cancer Cause, an organization that fundraises to educate the population about the dangers of oral cancer. She donates her time to these and countless other worthwhile events.

I've never met a woman who supports other women like Linda. In fact, as her protégée, one time (and ONLY once!) a meeting planner selected me rather than her for a particular event. Linda was authentically happy and proud of me, as only a mentor and "mother" can be! She found it validating, and, over the years, I've had a number of clients and meeting planners share with me that Linda has told them I'm a better "woman for the job" than her. While it was never true, she always lifted me up to others—even if it came at a cost to her. She was never threatened by my success, or the success of any of her peers or the women (and men!) she mentored.

Linda set the bar very high for me, and I know that I, and countless others, owe our success to her. She sets a standard that very few can emulate. I can only hope, through her example of grit, determination, and unparalleled passion, that I am able to continue to represent her spirit, generosity, and philosophy as I continue on this path she's paved for me. Read this book and you will truly understand all that is available to you if you are willing to work hard, get out of your own way, and take risks.

I'm sad for those who will never benefit from her expertise directly, but Linda should take great pride in knowing that people all over the world are better for having heard her and embraced her wisdom. The people who have been fortunate enough to cross paths with her will forever be better off because of her. This is her legacy; read this book, and embrace the wisdom she so freely gives!

Char Sweeney, CDPMA
Sweeney & Associates
www.charsweeney.com

Chapter 1

Meager Beginnings

Back in the 40s when I was born, most babies were delivered at home by a midwife. According to my mom, having me—her third child—was complicated. She was a small woman, only five-foot-one. I was not only eight pounds, but breech. While Dad ran to get a doctor, the midwife stood by for the delivery...which would most likely happen before the doctor was there. Sure enough, I came into the world with a big push, but I was not breathing.

The midwife could not get me to breathe right away, so she laid me aside and started working on Mom. My mother, in her fear, yelled for her to do something. The woman then submerged me in a pan of water, which must have either been too hot or cold—because right then I started crying, and she knew I was going to make it. Mom said it was only a few seconds, but time stood still until she knew I was not a stillborn.

After my parents got married in December of 1937, they lived with my paternal grandparents and my grandmother's adopted parents. Everyone in the family called the latter "Aunt" and "Uncle." They lived in a home that Uncle and his brothers had built in the early 1900s. Daddy's sister Carolyn, who is younger than him by twenty-six years, still lives in that home in Morgantown, West Virginia with her husband, Bill.

Carolyn is my aunt, but she is two years younger than me. It was always as if she was one of *our* immediate family. My brother, Ted, was six when Carolyn was born. My sister, Patty, was four; I was two. Mom said that Ted went to first grade crying that day. When the teacher asked what was wrong, Ted said, "Mommy had a girl, then Mommy had another girl...and now *Grandma* had a girl." He so wanted a baby boy in the family—and two years later, our youngest sister Bobbie was born, so Ted really was outnumbered his entire life.

Story has it that times were very tough in West Virginia during the late 30s and early 40s. My father loved aviation and anything to do with airplanes. After having a few odd jobs and settling into a glass factory where my grandfather worked, Dad sent applications for working at what was then Glen L. Martin Aircraft in Baltimore. Surprisingly, my father, his father, and my mom were all offered jobs at the aircraft factory. In 1942, Aunt, Uncle, my grandfather Jason Estep, my grandmother Stella Brewer Estep, "Bud" (my father's nickname), Margaret (my mom), and their two children (Ted, age three, and Patty, age one) all headed for Baltimore.

I once asked my mom if it was difficult getting the entire family to leave their family home and relocate, which wasn't done as often back then as it is today. Her response was that my father—who was raised as a privileged little prince and the only child of a very modest family—usually got his way with most ideas in his family. They idolized their son, and therefore when he came up with the idea of a better/bigger life, it wasn't difficult to talk them into leaving the only home they knew in West Virginia.

They all lived in a three-bedroom house in Chesaco Park, Baltimore. Mom, Dad, and Granddad all went to work the day shift at Glen L. Martin's, while Uncle, Aunt, and my grandmother stayed home to do the chores and care for the children. Uncle and Aunt had no children of their own, so they loved living with our family. They had raised my grandmother as their own daughter when her mother had given her and her two sisters to different relatives after a divorce. So, for all intense purposes, they were our great-grandparents. I was born in August of 1943, and Uncle died when I was a few months old. Soon after his passing, my father was drafted into World War II. After much consideration and worry, the family moved back to Morgantown when I was ten months old. They tell me I left Baltimore in a basket full of clean clothes (my car seat).

In his three years in the Army, my father was stationed in the Philippines and Japan. We still have the letters he and Mom wrote back and forth during those years. When Dad was twenty-six and the father of three children, his mom gave birth to Carolyn, his baby sister. Grandma had lost two babies between having my father and Aunt Carolyn. Granddad sent him a telegram when Carolyn was born in October of 1945, saying he had a baby sister. Dad wrote back that it seemed odd to have a playmate now that he'd had three of his own! Soon after Carolyn was born, Dad was honorably discharged because he had three children.

I can remember that happy day when Daddy came through the front door; in fact, it is my very first memory. I was standing tall in a wooden dining room chair, with little black patent leather shoes and a frilly dress. Mom was beside herself with excitement, holding me on the chair for a better look. She, Grandma, and Aunt had been cooking all day. Ted and Patty were six and four, and played nearby. Granddad ran out to greet the taxi and again we were one big happy family, living in what we later called the "BIG house." After Carolyn was born, Granddad Jason had a second, smaller house on the adjoining lot built so he, Grandma, and Carolyn could have a home of their own. This left Aunt, Mom, Dad, and the three of us in the house that Uncle had built.

Recently, I was sifting through our old home addresses, and checked out the home at 1461 Centerhill Avenue in Morgantown online. I discovered that it was *not* the "BIG house" we thought it was. It is listed as 1,071 square feet. How in the world did six adults and two children live there before moving to Baltimore? No wonder Granddad built the second house after Carolyn was born. We must have been really crowded.

Mom told me that I slept in the crib until Bobbie was about two years old and took it over. I assume Bobbie had a bassinet until she outgrew it, and I moved out of the crib around age seven. My first year of school, Mom said I was such a sleepy head. After school, around 4 PM, they always found me in my crib sleeping until about 7 PM. Then they'd get me up, bathe, and feed me. Then back to bed I went! Maybe that's why I can go on less sleep as an adult. I stored up many hours the first seven years of my life.

The neighborhood kids all played on Centerhill Avenue, on Brewer Hill as it was called back then (on the outskirts of Morgantown). One of my first scary memories was when I was around five years old. Pat was seven, and Ted was nine. The "older kids" (ages seven to ten) like Willard, Marie, Pat, Ted, and Anna Ray were playing ball in Willard's backyard. Willard had the great idea that it might be fun to throw an empty gas can—with the lid on it—into the fire his father had built in a huge metal can to burn trash. I was thankfully in the house. We heard a big boom and saw kids flying backward into the dirt road in front of Willard's house and across the street from our side porch. Either they fell backward trying to run, or it blew them into the road. I remember all the women running to gather the kids, checking them for injuries. Willard had burns on his arm and the side of his face... it could have been much worse if the gasoline can had contained more than a few drops of gasoline.

Another childhood memory was playing with my friend, Johnny. He was a nice little boy about my age. We loved playing cars and trucks under my front porch, where green mold covered the soil in the dampness and made the ground soft enough to make roads, tunnels, and play for hours on end. Johnny had a red dump truck that I coveted. It had a lever on the side that made the dirt it hauled slide off the back. My car was a plain sedan that did nothing but run over the roads we built.

One day, Johnny forgot to take his truck home when his mom Leona called to him to come eat dinner. I decided I'd like to play with it the next day, so I took it into our house and didn't tell anyone he'd forgotten it.

When my mom asked whose truck it was, I said, "It's mine...Johnny gave it to me."

After questioning me further, she realized I was telling a fib about how it got into my toy box. I still remember Mom walking me to their house. She made me knock on the door and tell one of the sternest moms in the neighborhood that I stole Johnny's truck and I was returning it with an apology! I have never "borrowed" anything without permission again. What a lesson!

Linda (me) at about age 4 or 5

Lessons Learned in Early Childhood

Homecomings are exciting days (Dad's return from WWII).

If you play with fire, you will be burned.

Never take another person's belongings without permission.

Chapter 2

Off to the South

Let me take you on a little journey. I will outline how I grew from the meager beginnings to a life that gave me such joy at every juncture—even the struggling and tough years brought valuable lessons that later brought great joy. To become humble and successful, I feel that you must go through many trials and errors to arrive at your "happy place" in life. Looking back over the past seventy-four years, I truly would not trade my life for anyone else's. It has been and continues to be a great run.

In 1950, Dad—being the ever wanderer of better opportunities—was working for Dipple and Dipple Coal Company in Morgantown after the war. They were opening a new job site in southern West Virginia, and Daddy decided that after living with his parents for fourteen years, it was time to take the job transfer. Off went our part of the family on an eight-hour trek over horribly curvy mountain roads, toward the rest of my childhood years in the Freeman/Bramwell area. Eight miles south of Bluefield, West Virginia, it's in the heart of the Appalachian Mountains. To a little seven-year-old girl who was just beginning to read, it almost sounded like a foreign country. I also had a very northern (Morgantown/ Pittsburgh) accent. I was now among the most southern accents I had ever heard.

My first experience with bullying at school happened when bullying wasn't even a word in 1950. The kids in my class would gather around me in the cloak room or playground at school and tell me to *"Tolk!"*

"What do you want me to say?" I would shyly ask.

Their response was always, "Just *tolk."*

I knew by their snickers and encouragement to read in our reading circles that my accent was as foreign to them as theirs was to me! It didn't take me long to try to sound just like them so the teasing would stop. Instead of saying "hi," "five," "bye," and "nine" like they did up north, I quickly learned that the southern version and heavy southern accent fit in better. Within months, I "twanged" like the rest of them—and today still carry that heavy southern accent. Little did I know then, in twenty-eight years I would become a professional speaker. My voice would be heard in all fifty states and on four continents in my thirty-six years of speaking to large groups in the dental profession. As Zig Ziglar once said to the audience at a National Speakers Association conference, "Many famous speakers have an accent, so never be ashamed of yours."

Speaking of pride, some folks are not proud of their "roots" or home state. I loved growing up in West Virginia. Years later, I would discover that many people have misconceptions about my home state and make fun of people who dwell there. I would hear jokes such as, "Why can't you take a family photo in WV? Because every time the photographer says cheese, they all get in a straight line." That, of course, made fun of the people in WV who accepted commodities from the state in the form of butter, cheese, powdered milk, and cornmeal to make cornbread. While my dad had a job and we were never on welfare, I remember vividly that many of our neighbors gladly accepted commodities. My mom used to drive folks to get in those lines, and sometimes they shared her commodities with her. So, yes, they existed. Food stamps and food stamp cards have replaced them. Back then, no one ever looked down on families who needed help. It was a matter of survival for some families.

There were other jokes, too. "How can you tell a rich West Virginian? By the number of wrecked cars in their front yards"; "The toothbrush was invented in West Virginia, because if it was any other state it would be called a teethbrush." Or, "What do a divorce and a tornado have in common in West Virginia? Somebody's going to be losing a trailer."

I'll admit that some of the jokes are a bit funny and maybe a little true, but I am here to tell you that many very smart and successful people are from West Virginia. In fact, our little town of Bramwell had the high school moniker of Bramwell Millionaires. In the early 1900s, with a population of less than 800 people, there were between twenty-five and thirty millionaires living in our town. These were mostly coal barons who had come from England, Wales, and Germany to settle first in Pennsylvania and then in the coalfields of Southern West Virginia. A *National Geographic* article in the 1950s revealed that some fifty years before the article was published, people called Bramwell "the richest little town in America."

I can also attest to the fact that some of the nicest and most caring people are from West Virginia. The children had the entire town behind them in sports and academics, and had the freedom to run and play since everyone looked out for all the youngsters. The only time this backfired was that if you did anything wrong, your parents knew about it before you got home. Discipline back then was very straightforward. We were expected to obey rules at home, school, and in our community. You were expected to do chores and your schoolwork, and then play. We were taught manners and respect.

Dads and moms were the kings and queens of the castle—and the children knew who was in charge. Children were loved, but trained to feel a certain level of gratitude and "privilege" to be able to have a roof over our heads, food in our stomachs, clothes to wear, and schools to attend. In today's world, with so many out of control youngsters in about 40% of households, I see way too often the child treated as the king or queen. They are the center of everything and told how great they are from day one. By the ninth grade or so, they believe they are the top of everyone's universe and their parents are Class B citizens, placed there to be at their beck and call, servicing their every want or desire.

While our parents loved and cared for us, we were *not* the Class A citizens of the household. For that, I am thankful. Nothing was handed to us—we had to earn it. We also learned coping and survival skills in tough times. Now, parents who have given too much and those who have become slaves to their children ask, "Where did we go wrong?" and "Why are we not getting the respect and appreciation we deserve?" Later in life, they ask, "Why can't our children cope and make better choices for themselves?" Putting parents back in the castle as heads of the household and drivers of the bus (versus passengers) keeps families moving in a forward and positive direction.

I love children, and would do anything for my children and grandchildren—but thankfully, both our children and granddaughters are respectful, hardworking, and have coping skills. Did we ever clash? Yes, we were their parents—not their best friends. Do we still disagree sometimes? Yes—it could be political views, lifestyle differences, or opinions that don't mesh. And if I see them doing something that is not in their best interest, I still speak up. That's what parents do, no matter the age of the child or grandchildren, because we love them and want the best life possible for them.

Are we dysfunctional? Yes—all families are from time to time. If we were perfect, we'd be in *Ripley's Believe It or Not!* Before my husband Don and I got married at eighteen back home in West Virginia, our old minister, Dr. Eastwood, gave us some advice. He said, "When couples tell me that they have been married for twenty-five years and never had one argument, I think to myself, 'Then you have never had any ideas!'" Families will argue and disagree and have differences in opinions, which is healthy. But holding grudges, blaming, and having anger toward one another fuels an unhealthy flame.

Lessons Learned in Elementary School

The classmates in second grade who made fun of my accent became some of my best friends.

We kids did not make the same mistakes twice. We grew from discipline by those in charge.

Based on income, we were money poor—but we had things that mattered. Poor, but proud.

We grew up with an attitude of gratitude for parents, teachers, and the law.

Chapter 3

Working Hard to Play Harder

When school let out for the summer, we kicked off our shoes and rarely put them back on until school started again in September. For us growing kids, between seven and fourteen, that meant a new pair of shoes in a different size at the end of every summer. We'd get a lot of stubbed toes and injured feet every summer, but all the moms kept band aids and that magic red medicine that didn't burn (mercurochrome). We also rarely went home after breakfast until suppertime at 5 PM. All the moms kept a loaf of white bread, peanut butter, and jelly for sandwiches, and a big plastic jug of Kool-Aid. Whoever's home we were closest to at lunchtime fed the neighborhood kids, who could number from five or six to ten or more. We have such fond memories of swinging on grape vines on the cemetery hill, jumping rope, playing ball, making huts on the riverbanks with woven weeds, and playing school on our front steps. Today, sadly, children can't enjoy the freedom we enjoyed.

One of my most memorable summer adventures includes my big brother Ted, who was going to teach me to ride a bike at age nine or so. Dad had bought me a used bike for fifteen dollars, and I was ever so proud of it. I polished it after every outing and put it in the basement in case it rained. Ted and I went beside the railroad tracks, since that was the only flat place in town. I did well, until I started going too fast—and had not learned how to apply the brakes. Over the river bank I went. Thankfully, the tall weeds tangled in the bike spokes and threw me over the handlebars. I landed inches from the river.

From ages seven to twelve, I loved living next door to Mr. and Mrs. Nowlin in Freeman. They had two grown children. Dorothy was married to a Navy career man. Arnold, the Nowlin's son, was in the Air Force. This wonderful couple relied on neighborhood kids to do odd jobs around their beautiful home. Ted had an afternoon paper route at age twelve to make extra money, and he also cut Mr. Nowlin's grass in the summer months, or shoveled the sidewalks after it snowed. If Ted had better things to do in the afternoon like play ball or ride bikes with Rodney, he would "hire" Pat and me to deliver his newspapers to about thirty homes.

He "paid" us with fudgesicles from Queen's grocery store, which were about a nickel back then. Treats were not plentiful, so we gladly obliged. Pat and I were ten and eight, not old enough to have a real job yet. I later started helping Ted by using scissors to trim grass from the sidewalks after he cut the grass at Mrs. Nowlin's. All for twenty-five cents per hour. Blisters and all, I was happy to be earning some spending money too. A few years later, at about age ten, I had the best job ever with Mrs. Nowlin. She asked me to wrap all her Christmas gifts for a few dollars. I loved seeing the beautiful gifts she selected for her family members. She also bought the most beautiful bows and wrapping paper. I could also count on hot chocolate and homemade cookies at her kitchen table.

After earning money from Mrs. Nowlin, I had the money-making "bug." I was about ten and loved looking through the Sears catalog, dreaming about the many things I'd buy if I had money of my own. My first entrepreneurial experience was just around the corner. While doing our Saturday chores and vacuuming Mom and Dad's bedroom, Pat discovered (and shared with me) Mom's only vice: *True Confessions* and *True Story* magazines hidden under Mom's side of the bed. The interlude into racy women's magazines was likely the *only* aversion for a 1950s mom from her everyday chores of cleaning, washing and ironing clothes, and preparing meals all day long.

Pat's job was to clean the downstairs living room, dining room, kitchen, and our parent's bedroom. My job was to clean the three bedrooms and bathroom upstairs. Pat was up by 8 and had her work done to go play by 11. Knowing I needed my beauty rest, I was just getting up around 10:30. I knew I could not go play until the work was completed. I remember Pat yelling at me for making dust fall from the upstairs hallway onto her vacuumed floors below.

Not only did Pat find the magazines, but we decided at our age we needed to learn a bit about love and boyfriends. So, we took Mom's magazines onto the coalhouse roof that slanted toward the back alley, so Mrs. Nowlin's watchful eye couldn't find us. It was not really dangerous, since it wasn't that far off the ground—and we could climb the apple tree to get up and down. Eating green apples until we had stomachaches and reading those magazines was one of that summer's best pastimes.

We found a small ad in the back of those magazines, which detailed how anyone could become a business person by ordering tins of white salve for sixty-five cents, then selling them for a dollar. The cream came in a silver tin with a bumble bee and clover on the top lid. I had no idea what the salve was used for, but assumed it was something like Vaseline for bee stings, mosquito bites, burns or poison ivy, etc.

Gee, I thought, *if I could only save enough money to order my first dozen, I could earn a whopping $4.80. I only need $7.80 to get started.* I just knew that once I started selling it, I could order more—every household would have some. Back in our day, it was safe for little girls to knock on doors or go door-to-door, borrowing or returning a cup of sugar or flour if our mom ran short in the middle of making something. I was ready to become a saleslady! I talked Mom into loaning me two dollars to add to my yard money, knowing I'd only profit $2.20 after paying Mom back. At least I could get started. I ended up selling forty-eight tins over that summer, making a profit of $16.80 (actually, $14.80 after paying Mom back). I knew we were getting ready to move to Bramwell—and I wouldn't know anyone there—so the timing for that summer job was great.

Another adventure at age twelve was moving from Freeman to Bramwell in seventh grade, and playing with classmates who went the opposite direction from the schoolhouse each afternoon. I missed our playmates in Freeman, the fun of the cemetery hill, the river bank, helping Mrs. Nowlin, and walking to Beet Hale's store for an occasional candy or ice cream, but I enjoyed the new fun in Bramwell.

Lessons Learned From Ages Seven to Twelve

Children developed imaginations (no toys or technology, so we created our fun).

Money did not grow on trees and was not handed to us... we had to earn it.

Sneaking magazines was okay—as long as we returned them to their place. Finding them gave me my first sales experience.

Chapter 4

The Magical Years in Bramwell

Our next home in Bramwell was three miles away from Freeman. Bramwell was, and still is, the magical little town that it was back in the early 1900s. It had three-story mansions—some with ballrooms or pools—stone churches with stained glass windows, elegant flower gardens, brick main streets, a couple stores, a movie theatre on Main Street, and a gas station. As a teen, I roller-skated with Brenda, and fished off a little man-made dam in Keesling Gardens—usually running all the way home yelling, "Look what I caught!" so Ted could take the fish off the hook for me. Most of the fish were so small, but who cared? I was proud of my catch.

I also shared "boy crush" stories and diaries with Kay. I remember walking across the swinging bridge to Kay's house on the other side of Bluestone River. The Corner Shop that Kay's father and mother opened around that time (mid 50s) remains a mainstay in Bramwell some sixty years later—though it has been owned by several others during the years. We still visit The Corner Shop when we visit Bramwell. It was a great business opportunity for Kay's parents at the time, and it gave school teens a place to go to dance and spend endless hours together. Most of the teens went to church, and parents did not have to worry about alcohol and drugs. I'm sure some of the boys sneaked off to play pool, or drink a few beers, Boone's Farm wine, and a little moonshine back in the day—but for the most part, high school kids were interested in education, sports, music, and their futures.

Many childhood and younger year bumps in the road shape us. During those bumps, we are not aware they are creating who we become as adults. Two important traits we can have are humility and self-esteem. Humility is having a low level of one's own importance—or being in awe of others who have done great things, never realizing others may admire us as well. Self-esteem is confidence in one's worth and self-respect.

In elementary school, Mrs. Thacker, my Sunday school teacher, knew that I loved seeing the pretty dresses Sherrie and Donita wore to school. I wore many hand-me-downs and rarely had a new dress, except at Easter. Mrs. Thacker taught us that it was best to say, "One day, I'd like to have a pretty dress like theirs," versus "I wish I had that dress." She also taught us that we "should never hide our talents under a bushel!" In elementary, I knew of no talents that I had, but that message never left me. Sharing the things I've learned over the years has been a great passion of mine. Today, we call it mentoring.

<u>Some of my most memorable lessons in humility and self-esteem were</u>:

In the 50s, it was not only *okay* that teachers and parents spanked children; it was totally acceptable and commonplace. Pat, Ted, and I knew that if we got out of line and did something wrong, we could be spanked—receiving a belt to the backside or a switching. While they didn't spank us often, our parents and their parents believed "If you spare the rod, you spoil the child!" Bobbie was five years younger than me. She was quite mischievous, but because she was the baby, she got by with much more than the three older kids.

My most memorable public spanking was in the sixth grade by my teacher, Mr. Fritz. Math was hard for me—especially that year. He gave us four math questions on a test and said he would give us all one whack with a paddle in front of our classmates for each math problem missed. To my dismay, I missed two of the equations—so I was scheduled on a certain day the following week for my public paddling.

I remember that day vividly. I wore a gold corduroy gored (full) skirt with all my crinoline petticoats, and Pat's that she'd loaned me. Sure enough, I felt nothing through all those clothes. The paddle got tangled in the crinolines that wrapped around it. Mr. Fritz was so mad that he gave me a third whack. I thought for sure I'd feel humiliated in front of my classmates, but others missed one to four so I didn't feel so bad—quietly amused that the crinoline petticoats saved me.

In ninth grade, I wanted to try out for majorette. In order to be a majorette, the rule in Mr. David Richardson's band was that you also had to be part of the concert band, which meant playing a musical instrument. Even though my father and brother Ted were great self-taught musicians and played guitar, and even though Pat played the clarinet in band, I was not keen on being in the concert band. I decided the clarinet would be the instrument I played, too. While I squeaked my way through concert band, I tried out for majorette and made it! Ted was on the sidelines that day in the gymnasium, lovingly calling me "spider legs "in front of his friends (I was very skinny). But thankfully, the judges didn't hear him. I loved practicing my baton and marching each day at band practice in downtown Bramwell.

When I tried out for majorette, I knew I had some stiff competition. Sherrie, Donita, Kay Rigney, and I were all ninth graders, and some of our competitors were upper-class gals. There were four openings, and all four of us made it. We were so thankful to Pam Haynes for helping us learn the routines. She was two classes above us and a great mentor. Trying out for head majorette was tougher two years later, as my best friends were all trying out. I knew no matter who won, three of us would be disappointed. I practiced nonstop, and by pure luck and dedication, I made it—but also felt bad for my friends who did not. I became quite proficient at twirling the fire baton between my junior and senior year. I still remember our blue and gold yarn boot tassels, handmade to match our uniforms. My mom attended all the basketball games where I did a solo fire baton act at halftime. She embarrassed me by carrying a quilt to roll me in if I accidentally caught my tassels on fire during the routine.

In my senior year, our band director Mr. Richardson encouraged me to go to Bluefield and try out for the Miss Bluefield 1961 Pageant. If I won, I could go on to the Miss West Virginia competition and get a scholarship to West Virginia University. Back in the day, I knew college was out of the question. Being the third of four children in a family with little money, I pretended I did not want to go to college because I knew it was not an option. For the boys in our community, graduating meant joining the military or going to work in the coal mines. For the girls, it was going to work for the FBI in DC—which recruited many of our high school graduates—or getting a job at the bank, dime store, or anywhere else that might be hiring.

I was very skinny and had no chance of winning a beauty pageant, but I knew I had a great talent with the fire baton. So, I talked my friend Brenda Painter into going to Bluefield for tryouts with me. Brenda had the right body, and I had the fire baton—if only I could have combined the two. My mom drove us for the tryouts eight miles away. Even though we were Bramwell girls, they let us register. When Brenda and I saw the other twenty-eight gals— some of who were from Concord College in Athens—we knew we were doomed. By this time, Brenda finked out and decided not to try out! I swore her and my mom to secrecy, making them promise that they wouldn't tell a soul we went to Bluefield that night to try out. There could only be fifteen finalists, and I knew I was not one of them.

Lo and behold, I received a call on Monday that I was to be back in Bluefield for photos and talent tryouts the next evening after school. The tryouts were slow, and by 11 PM it was finally my turn! As fate would have it, my fire baton was outlawed by the Fire Marshall rules, because I might have caught the velvet curtains in the auditorium ablaze. So, there I was...signed up for a pageant in three nights with no real talent. What was I to do?

Back in the 50s, we had color wheels that projected colored lights onto silver aluminum Christmas trees. I borrowed my dad's color wheel and did a slow dance routine with my regular baton—aluminum on the rubber tips—to the tune "Over the Rainbow." Needless to say, I did not make it to the top five—but I was glad I stuck it out for the duration. Some twenty years later, my teenage son, David, saw the photos in an album from my high school days. He said, "Mom, you were the prettiest of those ugly girls in that pageant." Thanks, David! If you want the truth, ask your teenage kids...

Always being a romantic at heart, I had a secret boyfriend from the second to fifth grade. His name was Mark, and he lived on the same Freeman street and played in our group—but of course he never knew I existed. Years after we graduated high school, his mom told me that he had written my name with chalk on their basement wall. The information came too late, because I was now in the sixth grade and liked Dorwin—a polite young man and my skating buddy at the roller rink. Again, he did not know I liked him, so I moved on to our preacher's son, Walter. Walter sat with me in church in the eighth grade, but nothing ever became of us, either. Oh, those girlhood crushes...they make me smile now, especially as I remember some of Kay's advice. She'd always say, "One day our prince in shining armor will appear."

In my sophomore year, Donnie Miles—one of the star basketball players—became our drum major. I immediately knew I did not like him, because he was tough...and wouldn't let the majorettes chew gum! I remember writing in my diary that year that "Donnie Miles thinks he is SOOOOO smart!" Months later, Pat and I were walking up the schoolhouse hill to church one Sunday evening. Pat paused and said, "Let's wait and walk with Donnie Miles."

The preacher's son had moved away, so that summer—when I was fourteen and Don was fifteen—we became friends who sat together in church. I watched him play basketball, and we met at the Corner Shop on Friday nights to dance to the 50s jukebox and have a cherry coke. Don was raised by his sweet grandmother, Granny Miles—her twelfth after eleven of her own children. He was smart, a bit shy, and funny. We "dated" all through high school. In our small town, girls outnumbered the boys two to one. So if you found your steady in the ninth grade, you never let them go. Otherwise, you went to the prom alone. On November 4, 2017, we will celebrate our fifty-sixth wedding anniversary! How can that be?

When I look at my beautiful granddaughters—Amy and Taylor, who are now twenty-six, and Jordan, who is twenty-three—I can't imagine them being married at eighteen, having a baby at twenty and a second baby at twenty-three. But back then, if you were twenty-three and not married, you were an old maid! My parents were fifteen and seventeen when they got married, so at eighteen, I felt very grown up.

Lessons Learned in My School Years

Clarity: Follow the rules of parents, teachers, and those in authority.

Commitment: Many a day during the winter months, we four children saw our dad come home from work with his work clothes frozen to his body. Dad was a strip miner who ran a huge Link Belt shovel on the side of a mountain, stripping the coal and dropping it hundreds of feet below to the coal trucks. Can you imagine this once privileged prince, now married with four children by the age of thirty, when growing up he never had to worry about anyone? No wonder Daddy enjoyed his beer and guitar on the weekends.

Competition: Mom always reminded us that not everyone can win...but you win by trying!

Compassion: The fifth grade teacher at our school, Mrs. Heltzel, brought her elderly mom from the UK to live in our town after Mrs. Heltzel's husband died; they were our next-door neighbors. At age fifty-five, Mrs. Heltzel died, and her mom, the eighty-something Mrs. Morgan, had no one. She did not drive, so we brought her mail from the post office. Ted cut her grass, and whichever girl took over her Sunday dinner did not have to do wash and dry dishes—so I *always* volunteered! Talking to lonely

Mrs. Morgan gave me compassion for others, especially the elderly; it also gave me listening skills as she talked for hours, as well as patience.

When I was in the tenth grade, Dad and four of his coal mining buddies accepted a position with J.A. Jones Construction out of Charlotte, North Carolina. They were contracted to build a dam in Baghdad, Iraq, so he was gone for twenty-seven months—arriving back home right after my high school graduation and before my wedding in November of 1961. Even though we missed Dad, those two years were fun years, because our mom was truly a kid at heart. She loved her four children and their friends. She'd never really had much of a childhood, as my grandfather drank a lot and was not always nice to his wife and children. Mom said she'd had to quit school in the eighth grade, since her father didn't believe girls needed an education. Plus, she'd needed to take in ironing and earn her way. She was also beaten a few times for going to church.

No wonder she married my dad at fifteen—and thank goodness his family loved her like a daughter. She was such a great mom, and she had fun with us. We went sleigh riding in the winter and swimming in the summer. We had slumber parties at our house, and she chaperoned school trips. The money Dad sent home from Iraq was tax-free, and three times what he would have made in West Virginia. Mom may not have had book smarts, but she was smart beyond words. She was also a daredevil who rode roller coasters with her grandchildren later in life and got her pilots license at age forty-seven while she and my dad were in California. They came to visit us in CA when Don was stationed in Madera. LaDona was born in December 1963, and Mom and Dad ended up staying in CA fifteen years. Dad owned a Cessna, and Mom decided that on cross country trips back to Virginia, she needed to be able to land the plane in case Dad had a medical emergency.

NOTE: In Bramwell every year for the past thirty years, Mayor Lou Dawson Stoker and her daughters, Dana and Jonnie, host The Bramwell Reunion. If you ever attended school or lived in Bramwell, you are compelled to "return to your roots" the last weekend in June. It is the school, family, and town reunion no one wants to miss. Well into her eighties, Mayor Lou looks fifty and has the energy of a teen. She's done more to keep the spirit of Bramwell alive than any other person. Thanks, Mayor Lou and girls. Check out the Bramwell Facebook page to see how the little town is still going strong more than 100 years beyond its golden era in the early 1900s.

Chapter 5

Seasons of My Life

In the book *Passages*, the author Gail Sheehey talks about the stages of life. She says that the first twenty years of life are the springtime; the second twenty years (age twenty to forty) are the summer. From ages forty to sixty is the autumn, and sixty to eighty is the winter—a planning time for the long hibernation called end-of-life status.

I tend to believe that with the new lifespan—as many live to be well over a hundred—it is more like twenty-five-year segments in today's measurements. In my retirement years, in addition to co-founding Oral Cancer Cause (oralcancercause.org) in 2012, I have taken on several volunteer jobs, advisory board positions, and committees at church. One of these is volunteering to drive residents of the Sullivan House (Virginia Beach independent apartments for the elderly) to attend medical/dental appointments, see friends or relatives close by, or go to the store. Many of the residents use walkers, so riding the Hampton Roads Transit bus is not an option for them.

Recently, I drove a sweet little lady to visit a friend who had been her director of nursing at a local hospital some sixty years ago. The lady I drove (in her eighties) was then a young bride/nurse from Haiti who was married to a young doctor from their country. The friend that she asked me to take her to see lived in Virginia Beach with her friend's daughter. That sweet little friend is one hundred and five, sharp as can be. She makes her own bed and dresses herself daily. So, my new measurement for life is that spring is the first twenty-five years; summer is twenty-five to fifty; autumn is fifty to seventy-five; and over seventy-five is winter. It's nice to know at seventy-four I have not yet entered the winter. My new goal is to live to be more than a hundred like Josephine—but only if I can retain my health and mind!

Linda (me)/Josephine/Janine

My springtime included my birth in Baltimore, and growing up in northern West Virginia the first seven years then southern West Virginia until age eighteen. It included dating my sweetheart, Don, all through high school. Getting married at our church with a hundred guests (a big crowd for a small town) on November 4, 1961. Don's early Air Force days, and being transferred to Madera, California—and two years later becoming a twenty-year-old mom to a beautiful baby girl, LaDona. Then, a move to Mobile, Alabama, and becoming a mom again at twenty-three to a tiny baby boy, David.

To say the springtime of my life was the happiest is so true—except they were truly hard years as well. Don's career field (radar technician) took him to several remote and unaccompanied tours for a year or longer, which meant the children and I were alone for many of his twenty-one Air Force career years. Being alone became a way of life for many military wives. I enjoyed the wives' club, and sharing babysitting with other wives who needed to go to doctor's appointments or the commissary. I also loved being a mom. I did all my housework, laundry, sewing, and letter-writing after 8 PM. The years that I did not work when the children were younger meant we could play, go to the pool or beach, or hang out with other military moms and children.

Looking back over the past fifty-six years since I was first hired in a dental practice, I realize the value of on-the-job training. As a graduate from high school, knowing college was not an option due to no money, I originally planned to go to Washington, DC like so many of my classmates and start my career as a secretary for the FBI. I had been dating Don since the ninth grade. He enlisted in the Air Force in April of my senior year, and planned to come home after basic training in six weeks. After having gone through the interview and the background check conducted by the FBI, I decided that if I went to DC, I might change my mind—and the life Don and I had planned together would be off. I was totally disappointed when I found out I would not see Don for six months. He had a high score in radar technology, and was sent to Biloxi, Mississippi to school. They had an immediate opening in the class that was starting right away, so on to Plan B.

I needed a job, so I planned to go to the bank and start my business career there. The only problem was that the bank would not even interview prospective employees until they were eighteen—and that was an entire summer away. I went to Lynchburg, Virginia to visit my brother and sister-in-law and help out with their year-old baby. While there, my mom called to tell me that a dentist in Bluefield needed to hire a receptionist/assistant to help out in his office. After three weeks in Lynchburg, I went back home; right after the Fourth of July, I started my career in dentistry in July 1961.

I was very lucky to work for a wonderful dentist in Bluefield, Dr. Jim Nelson. The $1 per hour ($125 per month) for four and a half days per week was a big increase in salary from the fifty cents per hour I'd made afterschool babysitting Randy Gibson, who was seven. My sister had been his babysitter until she had gone to nurse's training in Cincinnati, and I'd taken the job in eleventh grade. Randy's mom Areta was a classy, elegant, beautifully-dressed bank employee. She became one of my role models of becoming a businesswoman one day.

Although I spent a lot of time pretending I didn't want to go to college—secretly knowing that as the third of four children, there was no money for me to go—I eventually realized that I really did *not* want to go. First, I watched my brother drop out of West Virginia University after one year due to finances. Even though he lived with our grandparents during his year there, money was very tight for books, etc., so Ted gave up his dream of becoming an aeronautical engineer. Pat went to Christ Hospital in Cincinnati on a nursing scholarship, then worked there for two years to pay it back. But I watched our mom cry many weeks when she did not have even five dollars to send Pat for spending money. I began to think school was okay, but it would slow me down from being the successful businesswoman I wanted to be. I knew algebra, geometry, and Latin would never be needed in the world I wanted to create.

Lessons Learned in My Springtime

Higher education is a must-have in most professions, but on-the-job training can lead to success.

Military guys don't always get to come home on leave when they think they will.

I was lucky to have a first real boss who was a gem of a teacher, who believed in me before even I did. I will always be eternally grateful to Dr. Jim Nelson for hiring me for four months, knowing I planned to be married soon. He gave me my start! I still have emails he sent me in his eighties before his death. Two of those are below:

December 2011:

Dear Linda,

Many years ago I saw in you something very special. Now to be able to see all that you have achieved brings such pleasure to me. My hope would be that as you are now changing directions in your life that you would be able to have some time to relax.

I think of you often and am so grateful to have been a part of your life and you a part of mine.

My sincerest congratulations to you and Don on your 50th wedding anniversary. I really treasure that wedding picture. Thanks for sending it.

With warmest regards,
Jim N.

June 2005:

Dear Linda,

Please accept my belated congratulations on being selected to receive the Distinguished Service Award at the Hinman dental meeting. A more deserving selection could not have been made as you take your place in this very exclusive group of Distinguished Service Award winners.

I am not at all surprised at your phenomenal success.

Please keep me up to date as I so look forward to hearing from you.

My very best,
Jim N.

Chapter 6

And Off We Go

Don and I were married on November 4, 1961, at our hometown church in Bramwell. Our first assignment was Biloxi, Mississippi, where Don was in the C shift at school (4 PM to midnight). After a two-day "honeymoon" fourteen miles from home, he left to go back to school. I had to wait a month to join him, until my allotment was intact and we had enough money for me to travel by bus to join him. I will never forget that Trailways bus trip to Mississippi. Sadly, segregation was still going on. Being from our small southern West Virginia town—where blacks and whites were the same—I had no idea that if I went into the bus terminal in Montgomery, Alabama half asleep at 4 AM and chose the bathroom for folks of color, I would soon realize I was not welcome in there. And they would not be welcome in the one for white people! That was very scary and foreign to me. Thankfully, it's not like that today.

Newly married, my allotment was $91.30 per month, and Don's paycheck as a one-striper was $33.50 every two weeks. When I tell our children and grandchildren we lived on $150 per month, they can't imagine! Back in 1961/62, you could find a tiny efficiency furnished apartment for $45 per month, and gasoline was about twenty-eight cents per gallon. We did not have to worry about gasoline, because for the first two years of our marriage, we did not own a car. Don had a ride to the base in our apartment carpool, and I walked to the nearest store or took a taxi if I went to the commissary once a month. I usually split the fare with Brenda Butler, from Tennessee—another Air Force wife in the apartments who also did not have a car.

Everyone who lived in the nine efficiency apartments enjoyed our closeness. The apartments were built into a three-story home, run by a wonderful Cajun French couple, Mr. and Mrs. Pavich—originally from Louisiana. Mrs. Pavich took delight in helping young Air Force wives learn some of her Cajun recipes. She also had a wash house with two free-standing wringer washers in the shed beneath the pecan trees. We military wives took turns using them on certain days.

My mom never let Pat or me use her wringer washer, since the heavy wringer part had a habit of swinging around mid-use—so Mom feared we would be injured. Mom did the washing, and we girls hung the wet clothes on the clotheslines. We also did some of the easy ironing. I still have faint scars on my abdomen from learning to iron at about age nine on the front porch in the summer, wearing shorts and midriff tops. I often got the iron too close to my body while ironing pillowcases. After learning how hot an iron was, I learned to stand farther away.

I had two laundry snafus while in Biloxi. One of our wedding presents was a white chenille bedspread. I knew that bleach kept things white and bright, so I bought a bottle of bleach to use on the spread. The problem was, I did not read the directions, and had not learned anything about laundry products. I put the entire gallon bottle of bleach in with only the chenille spread. I remember crying as Mrs. Pavich and I took the spread out in threads by the handfuls. I had no idea bleach could also ruin things if not used correctly! My other snafu was doing Don's uniforms. The fatigues were dark green and needed heavy-duty starch. We saved seventy-five cents per piece to do them ourselves versus sending them to the laundry. The steps were to dip the material into the starch, hang it on the line to dry, sprinkle it with water, and roll it up. Then, after an hour or so, we ironed each piece for a long time. They always came out well. We girls in the apartment building set up ironing boards and extension cords on the patio one day per week and had ironing parties. I wasn't working, so I had plenty of time to be domesticated.

But one morning, Don and Brenda's husband, Gary, had to be on the flight line at 5 AM for a parade in their khakis (beige pants and shirts). Little did I know, they were not supposed to have cuffs on the pants—so when I ironed the 505s, I cuffed Don's! Oh my, I do believe that was the first time in our marriage that he yelled at me. They were late and his slacks for an inspection were two inches too short! I think Brenda from next door ran over with Gary, grabbed the iron, put a towel on the table, and got the cuffs ironed flat before they missed their ride! After that, we paid the $1.50 and had the 505s done at the laundry.

Everyone in our apartment building wanted to get orders for California. Everyone put in for California on their "dream sheet," and most of them went to Tampa! Don put in for Langley Air Force Base in Hampton, Virginia—the closest one to home. We got Madera, California. We were ecstatic, as most young newlyweds might have been. In May of 1962, after a month home on leave, Don and I boarded the train for California. I remember both our moms, Margaret and Myrtle, standing on the train station platform being sad and worried. Don and I could not wait until that train pulled out. A new adventure was surely about to happen!

I think we had about $85 in cash—with our wedding gifts and clothes in eleven boxes—and off we went. We knew we would have to rent an apartment and pay for ground transportation once we arrived in California after the five-day train adventure, so we shared box lunches from the various stops along the way versus even thinking about the dining car. I remember in Clovis, New Mexico, we had the most beautiful ham and cheese sandwich, chips, and an apple to share. But as the train pulled out and we opened the sandwich, we realized the thick contents were a quarter of an inch wide on the part that showed, but the sandwich was three-fourths bread; it was wrapped to look thick and luscious, but it was an optical illusion! Of course, after the train pulled away from the station, what could the passengers who were duped do about it? At $5.50, that was a huge bit of our cash!

Arriving in Madera, we must have looked like two gypsies with all our "things." We took a taxi to the only hotel in Madera, and got settled into the room down a very long, dark, carpeted hallway. The hotel was old, but clean, with a nice shower. I think the room rate was $8 per night. Don was off the next morning to the base, and I was off on foot to buy a newspaper and start looking for an apartment in town. Luckily, I found a one-bedroom downstairs duplex on South H Street. It was in our price range of $45 to $50 per month, and was being vacated that afternoon at 1. Perfect.

We had just enough money to make it, but we did not know there was a $25 deposit to turn on the electricity in our name. We were not worried, though, since Don had a month of back pay ($65), and the first of the month was not too far away. When I explained the situation to the landlord—that we had no car and very little money until Don's back paycheck—he gladly let us pay a half-month's rent and drove me to the electric company to get that set up. When I think of how many locals along our path looked after the young military, it warms my heart!

Our next day brought bad news. At the radar site office, they could not locate Don's pay records. He could not get paid, and we had about $1.30 left after the electricity deposit, the half-month rent, and the taxi that had charged me double because of our eleven boxes! So here I was in the apartment, but I didn't want to unpack our things until I cleaned the shelves and appliances, and then moved in properly. The people before us had been mopping the floor when the landlord and I drove up to take a look. It was not dirty, but was not as clean as I could make it—if I only had some cleaning supplies! I remember at the grocery store we bought a package of cheese (eight slices), a loaf of bread, two cans of soup—and that would hopefully sustain us that weekend.

Being broke 3,000 miles from home and not knowing where the next meal might come from, we did what most young people do: Don called his mother. She agreed to wire $30 (which would be like $300 in today's world, based on her meager earnings as a cashier at Piggly Wiggly in 1962). Don had a ride to the base with a backyard neighbor that Monday morning, and I was off to the Western Union office about ten blocks away so I could be there when it opened. My goal was to get the money and go buy cleaning supplies and two pillows so I could go home and unpack the boxes for our little duplex. The following week, I was going to look for a job—hopefully with a dentist in Madera close enough to walk to work. Back then, there were only four dentists in town.

I arrived at the Western Union office and told the gentleman I was Linda Miles, and my husband and I were expecting to have a message with $30 from back home. I'm sure he noticed the anxiety that I had from not knowing if the wire had come in one day or several. As he ran through the tape on his machine, I thought to myself, *Please, go slower. You might miss it.*

Finally, the very last message was from Myrtle. "But," he explained with a frown, "it's in your husband's name, so I can't give you the money."

Tears had always worked well for me in situations like this, so I cried! He was noticeably upset for making me cry, and asked if I had a number at the radar site at Raymond. I didn't, of course, since we didn't rely on phones like we do today. He was so kind that he looked it up, then called and located Don.

"Yes," Don said. "By all means, give her the money."

I think that was our lowest day of being fearful we might not make it. Even though I wasn't terribly hungry, I walked into a cafe on Yosemite Ave and ordered the best breakfast of pancakes, maple syrup, and bacon I think I have ever enjoyed. Then, I went to buy supplies to go make our first real home in California. I also had ironing to do from all the days the clothes had been packed. Thankfully, there was an ironing board in the broom closet, and I had an iron. I also wanted to make a special dinner for Don. Later, after meeting others in our neighborhood who were also young Air Force and civilian couples, we laughed at how—if we had known them—we could have borrowed a few potatoes and such when we thought we were going to go hungry. In time of need, military folks have a language and understanding only they can fully comprehend.

I applied for jobs at all dental practices, but no one was hiring. They were especially *not* going to hire an Air Force wife whose husband was at the radar site, since they knew our time there might be less than eighteen months.

Not even a dentist named Dr. Miles would hire me! So, I gave up on staying in dentistry—at least while in Madera.

One day in the neighborhood, one of the Air Force wives talked about how she had helped her grandmother in a nursing home back in Ohio. While I did not have any nurse's training—or know anything about caring for medically-compromised patients—Sondra gave me some tips about how easy it was to bed bathe bedbound patients by washing one limb at a time. She also said she changed the linens on beds with patients still in them. She rolled the patient to one side, placing the clean sheets over half of the bed, then rolled them onto the clean side to make the other half.

I was intrigued. *Well, it's still health care,* I thought. *I love people, so why not apply for a job as a nurse's aide?* I did just that at Dearborn Hospital, in town. It was a forty-bed, private hospital—and the only one within twenty to thirty miles from the larger hospital in Fresno. To my surprise, they hired me. My wage was about $200 per month, which was more than the $125 a month I'd made in Bluefield the four months I'd worked in dentistry. I walked about seven blocks to work at 6 AM, many mornings before daylight. It was good to get off at 3 PM. The head nurse, Marianne Paulo, was a pretty redhead who looked like Lucille Ball—and she had a stern, yet kind, demeanor. She assigned me to more experienced aides like Martha and Mary, who were in their forties. Alice Villarreal and I were the two youngest, and we became fast friends. I worked at Dearborn for fourteen months, until it was time to give birth to our baby girl.

Our wedding day 1961
Mr. & Mrs. Miles

Lessons Learned as a Young Air Force Bride

Budget training becomes easy if you have little money for the first few years.

Parents should teach children basic skills like washing, ironing, budget shopping, and house cleaning.

Never put where you really want to go next on a military "dream sheet." It won't happen!

In finding a job: Where there's a will, there's a way.

Chapter 7

The Greatest Joy/Being a Mom

I had a fairly easy pregnancy after I got past the morning sickness, which was horrible. For a couple weeks, they were painting the walls of the hospital. When I arrived at 6:30 AM, in time for the morning huddle from the night shift staff, the paint smell mingled with the bacon they were cooking for breakfast. My stomach couldn't handle it, and I often ran straight to the ladies' room to throw up. My coworkers knew I was pregnant before the doctor confirmed it.

My parents were happy about the baby, but Don's mom, Myrtle, was not. She thought we were too young and too poor to have a baby until Don got out of the Air Force. She also was *not* keen about being a grandmother! But over the years, her grandchildren and great-grandgirls became her prized possessions. At that time, Myrtle did not know Don would be staying in the service for twenty-one years—and we didn't, either.

A year before I got pregnant, Don worked part-time at a service station near the hospital. With his extra income and my salary, we were able to buy our first used car in 1963: a 1957 white Pontiac with a blue stripe along the side. It was a beauty. We also moved into a two-bedroom duplex on Bloker Street, which was closer to the hospital, before the baby was born. Don was promoted twice in two years, and we were now "on our way." Then, in my eighth month, I learned the baby was going to be about eight pounds and breech. That meant I had to have a C-section. The doctor explained that first babies could be hard deliveries, and that the risk of breaking the baby's hip or shoulder warranted the C-section—which would be better for both mother and baby.

We called my parents that evening, as I was very scared. The baby was scheduled the nineteenth of December, in three weeks—right before Christmas. I asked my mom if she and Dad could come to California. But winter weather in West Virginia could be treacherous, and money was about as scarce for them as it was for us.

Mom said, "No, we can't even think about going to California, Linda. I wish we could, but I just know your dad will say no."

I asked to speak to my dad, and worked some magic with my tears. Eventually he sighed and said, "We will check into the train, and get back to you tomorrow." Since he was not working steadily during that month, running a Link Belt heavy duty shovel as a strip miner, and my parents had friends in south California they'd wanted to visit for years, he eventually conceded. "We will come," he told me. "And we may just decide to stay, if I can get work in California." Dad was all about taking care of his family and seeking a new adventure. I think I took after him, because I love new work opportunities.

Mom and Dad arrived in Madera two days before my scheduled C-section delivery. I was in the hospital until December 23. Soon after, we learned that Don had orders to leave in eight weeks for a fifteen-month Air Force assignment in the Philippines. The day after Christmas, Mom and Dad went to Los Angeles to visit their best friends, Kelsey and Dorothy Raber—who were also from West Virginia, but had moved to California some twenty years earlier.

My parents knew we needed quality bonding time as a family, with a new baby and a long separation on the horizon. Even though I was only twenty when LaDona was born, she became the focal point of my existence. Some new moms dread when their babies wake up at night. I loved every minute of caring for this sweet little baby—even the middle of the night feedings and diaper changes. I think I tormented my first baby by dressing her in cute little clothes and hanging rows of toys across her crib or playpen when the poor baby just wanted to sleep! She and I were soon to be on our own for one of Don's many years away. I knew it was going to be a long fifteen months, and hoped it went by quickly. With a first baby, you quickly learn this little person is totally dependent on you. I was up for the challenge. I now had a new baby, not much money, and a car that ran only sometimes. I became very grown up overnight.

Mom and Dad liked Los Angeles. Dad got a temporary full-time job as a repairman for the telephone company, and they rented a little two-bedroom house in Lynwood. There was no need for me to return to West Virginia, so I moved with the baby to Lynwood into one of my parents' two bedrooms. As it turned out, Dad was hired by Kaiser Steel in Eagle Mountain a year later. Mom had a job as a unit secretary at St. Francis Hospital. My two sisters had just had their first babies. Pat and her husband Buzzy lived in Kentucky. Bobbie and her husband Doug were in Lynchburg, near our brother Ted, his wife Charlotte, and their family. When the Iron Ore Mine in Eagle Mountain hired Dad, he and Mom moved to the desert when company housing became available.

Bobbie and Doug decided to come to California for a year—staying in Lynwood, sharing the rent with me, while the two of them finished school at night. I was able to go to work as a nurse's aide in the orthopedic department at St. Francis from seven to three. Doug had a full-time day job. Bobbie watched LaDona during the day, and I watched their baby, Kim at night. After fifteen months, Don came home, and everyone left Lynwood. We drove cross country in a newer model Chevrolet. Bobbie and Doug drove back to Lynchburg, near Ted and Charlotte, where they've all lived since. Pat and Buzzy also moved to Eagle Mountain, California when Kaiser hired Buzzy and Pat became the company nurse for the local iron ore mine family doctor. They eventually moved to Richmond, Virginia.

Mom and Dad stayed in Eagle Mountain another fourteen years. They attributed the visit to see us in Madera as the turning point for them financially. Dad was able to retire from Kaiser at fifty-nine, and Mom retired from the post office with a good retirement as well. They moved back to a little Timberlake house in Lynchburg, Virginia—near Ted's and Bobbie's families.

Lessons Learned in Pregnancy and Early Motherhood

When all else fails, tears work well with dads.

We should have our first babies over again and give them a second chance!

House and childcare sharing is the best way for young families to make it while starting out.

Chapter 8

Life as a Military Wife and Mom

Don's homecoming from the Philippines when LaDona was fifteen months old was exciting yet frustrating. Without cell phones back then, and no pay phones on a military flight line, I could only hope that Don would get on the first military flight standby from the Philippines to the Travis Air Force Base, San Francisco. He was then booked to catch a civilian flight to Los Angeles, and all I knew was his "anticipated" arrival time. Without any way to communicate that he did not make it, we headed off to the LAX airport with LaDona, all dressed up to meet Daddy. We went not once, but *three* times—as he kept getting bumped from two other standby flights.

Finally, two days later, he made his connections, and we were off to LAX from Lynwood once more. I was so excited (again) as I exited my side of the car and went around to get LaDona from her flimsy little baby body strap as she stood in the middle front seat. I suddenly realized that I'd given her my car keys to play with since she was hot and fussy—and now she was locked in the car with them. I frantically tried to figure out a way to get her out as she chewed on the key ring and waved at me.

Thankfully, a man going to his vehicle saw me going from side to side and came to our rescue. He had a coat hanger in his car, and we were able to get into my car and get her out. By this time, LaDona was probably thinking, *Here we go again meeting someone who might not show up!* It was hard to explain to Don that because Bobbie and Doug lived with me, LaDona—hearing her little cousin Kim call Doug "daddy"—had begun to call Doug "daddy" too. She thought her "other daddy" was an eight-by-ten black and white photo of a young man in uniform. It did not take her long to become Don's buddy, but it was a bit daunting the first three days.

In March 1965, after packing up the 1963 Chevrolet— which I'd traded the Pontiac for a few months earlier— we were off to drive cross country from LA to West Virginia on leave, then on to our next duty station in Mobile, Alabama.

We spent three years in Mobile, and our son David was born in 1967. The day after David was born, Don got orders for Alaska. We were saddened that once again he would miss the babyhood of our second child, but so relieved his orders were not for Vietnam. In five months, he would be gone for yet another year. This time, Don went to the Aleutian Islands (Port Molar, Alaska), and would return when David was fifteen months old. I planned to stay in Mobile with the children, but had to move out of base housing to Parkway Apartments near the base for the year he was gone.

Parkway Apartments were right outside the base flight line, which made it convenient for the commissary, Base Exchange, medical clinic, and the pool. LaDona was almost four and David was a baby. The apartments had many wives of those in Vietnam, along with young civilian and Air Force couples. We relied on each other to babysit when we had commissary shopping or a doctor's appointment. With Don gone for a year, I decided I had nothing but time, so I took the children on the train from Alabama to California to spend Christmas and a few weeks with Mom and Dad. Going out, LaDona found a sweet little lady one seat over who knitted her Barbie dresses on the five-day trip. David was a great baby on the way to California, sleeping all night at five months old. No one even knew there was a baby onboard.

After being spoiled for six weeks at Mom and Dad's, plus being very constipated on the train ride back in late February, he cried a lot—so the trip back seemed to take twice as long. Don was due home in the fall, and we would be going to who knew where at the time. Two months before Don got home, we found out our next duty station was going to be Homestead Air Force Base in Florida. We all looked forward to being a family again, but little did we know at that time that being in a GEEIA (Ground Electronics Engineering Installation Agency) meant Don would travel nonstop to radar outposts up and down the east coast.

Soon after David was born, while still living in base housing in Mobile, I met Sharon Deas at a neighbor's "bra party." Sharon was putting her husband through college by selling bras! The Sculptress Bra Parties were a huge hit back in the 60s—much like Tupperware, but for ladies' lingerie. It was a very expensive lingerie line—bras were about $17-27. In today's world, that would be about $200 each. But these were magic bras, designed like the Golden Gate Bridge in San Francisco. All you had to do was bend forward, lift down the front part like a nursing bra, let all the fatty tissue from your rib cage and under your arms fill the bra cups, pull it back in place, and *voila*! The tissue would soon redirect, and you could add two to four inches to your bustline!

Since I'd worn a 32B padded bra all my life, and had just had a second baby, I was truly fascinated with the product when I saw women go into the fitting room with Sharon. She did the fittings along with her assistant, who wrote down the measurements of each guest. They wanted to make sure each custom-fitted bra was perfectly ordered. These women I knew walked out very bustier than when they walked in; and, of course, each woman there ordered not one but two of the bras! When I told Don that I wanted to sell the products, he was skeptical that this might not be a good business for me to get into. My argument was that after he returned home, I could hold the parties one evening per week while he was with the kids. Then I could be the stay-at-home mom I wanted to be during the day.

After he left again for a year and we moved off base to Parkway apartments, I went to my second bra party. I became even more convinced that if I loved the product, I could sell it. I called my dad—who also had an entrepreneurial mindset—and asked if he would loan me the money to start a business, which would be $125. He laughed and told all his friends at Kaiser he was in the bra business with his daughter. After two shows, I paid Dad back the $125 for the basic kit and had enough money saved for the down payment on my deluxe bra kit, which was $335. Don was away that year, and unaware I was in the business. I wanted to make sure it was going to succeed before I told him.

During our month on leave, I was selling bras, lingerie, and makeup the whole thirty days before Don reported to duty at Homestead Air Force Base in Florida (south of Miami/Gateway to the Keys). Not only did I have over $500 in checks to deposit, but I recruited two friends during that thirty-day leave at home. We rented a three-bedroom home in Leisure City near the elementary school. Two years later, we moved into base housing at Homestead Air Force Base. When I opened my business account, the bank teller handling my deposit said, "Well, you can't be an Avon lady, and these checks are too large to be Tupperware—what type of home parties do you do?"

I proudly announced that I sold the Sculptress Bras. She was so excited and told me that there was a woman in Miami who sold them, but she wouldn't come all the way to Homestead unless we could guarantee a $300 party. I told her that I would show these products to one woman or a dozen. She held my very first Homestead party, and from that, I was a District Director in three years and had sixty-seven women in my down line (direct and indirect recruits). I attended sales conventions for Con Stan and Nurti-Metics, the makeup component. At the time, it was an El Monte, California home-based company that was later bought out by their Australian division.

At twenty-nine, I was netting four to five times what a normal job would have paid in the early 70s. I had earned a pink LTD Ford, and had my name on the Holiday Marquee in Miami when I won the car. Our carport neighbor and an air policeman, Bill Cooper, told Don that his own wife had been very thin and small-breasted her entire life, but after the Sculptress Bras she'd turned into a new woman. He went on to say that if he and Don could invent jockey shorts that did as much for men as that bra did for women, they would be rich!

A couple funny things happened with the pink LTD. Don drove it to California to leave LaDona and David with my parents for four days, then he and I drove to Scottsdale for the Con Stan (Sculptress) Annual Convention. Try finding your pink LTD in a hotel parking lot with 500 of the same car there. When we filled it up later one afternoon, the gas station attendant said, "Where on earth are you driving this car? This is the fifth time today I've filled it up."

Why then, after six years, did I go back into dentistry as an endodontic assistant?

We loved living in southern Florida. After moving into base housing in 1970, I discovered the base would not allow me to hook an answering machine to my government base phone line. That meant I had to be home all day for the phone calls one gets when they have a busy business and recruits. I could no longer take the kids to the beach or park every day. Some of the women I recruited had way too many customer complaints—which I ultimately settled—and now that David was going to preschool, I longed to be back in a work environment with other adults. The money I made was great, and it would have been perfect if in direct sales you only had to take care of *your* customers. Putting out fires from others' mistakes drove me back to a normal job.

Louise, whose husband was stationed with Don, called and asked me if I could come and work for three weeks in the endodontic dental practice she worked with in Miami.

"Yes," I said. "But only if you tell the endodontist that I only worked in a dental office in Bluefield for four months before getting married in 1961. I'm really rusty."

Louise agreed that she would tell him—but she failed to do so, knowing he most likely would not have hired me for those three weeks while his assistant, Meredith, was out west with her parents. I'll never forget how inadequate I felt that first day when the doctor put his thumb in the air as a signal that he wanted the loop of the anesthetic syringe placed on his thumb to start numbing. For all I knew, he was thumbing a ride to Homestead! Thanks to this wonderful temporary boss and his patience, I made it through those three weeks, got paid my $86.24 per week, and fell back in love with being part of a dental team.

On Thursday of my third week there, he took Louise, my business assistant friend, my coworker Joanne, and me to lunch. Two things that he said that day taught me so much humility and self-esteem. He said that even though Meredith was coming back Monday, he'd enjoyed my work very much. Then he—not in a mean-spirited way—said how lucky we girls were to be in a profession like dentistry without a degree. We were, as he kindly went on to say, "respected healthcare professionals." We were lucky, because most "uneducated people work shift work and carry trays."

Those words, though given with respect, never left me. I might not have had a college education, but I was *not* dumb! When Meredith came back, the dentist asked me to help him two afternoons a week in the Homestead practice they were going to be using part-time. That was good for me, as I was still semi-engaged in the bra business. I also taught baton twirling to the Dependent Youth Activities on base on Wednesday afternoons, so Tuesday/Thursday afternoons in the practice were perfect.

One of my proudest moments came twenty years later. By that time I was working as a fairly well-known management consultant at age forty-nine. That same endodontic practice that I'd worked in from 1972-1974 as a new assistant, invited me back to do a full-blown consultation. Everyone else left the reception area where we were holding our all-day review of findings session to go to the breakroom for lunch.

My former boss just sat there, slowly shaking his head. When I asked if he was okay, he said, "I can't believe, listening to you this morning, that you could be the same young Air Force wife who was my assistant at twenty-nine."

I smiled and said, "I was actually this smart twenty years ago...but neither of us knew it!"

We had a great laugh over that! He was truly one of the kindest bosses anyone could have had—and smart beyond smart. One of my most memorable moments of the two years I worked in the endo practice was that only after a month of working there, my grandfather died on a Monday. Our family had to leave Wednesday for the funeral, and I missed three days of work. To my surprise, upon my return, my paycheck remained intact. I did not feel I deserved to be paid with so little time there, but it was a kind gesture that stayed with me my entire career. It helped me be a better employer when I had a team of ten in our corporate office years later. Compassion goes a long way in leaving an indelible mark on the employer/ employee relationship. My mom used to say, "I wish I could work for my daughter. She is so good to her employees." I would always remind her, "If it were not for those employees, I would not be where I am today."

In 1974, Don left for another year in Alaska, this time in Tin City (north of Nome). Not wanting to move off-base in Miami with a seven- and ten-year-old, I called my sister Pat and said, "How would you like having us move to an apartment in Richmond near you?"

Pat immediately sent me the names and phone numbers/ addresses of the only two endodontists in Richmond in 1972. I heard back from one of them and arranged an interview. We moved into a three-bedroom townhouse in west Richmond. I worked as an assistant for the endodontist Dr. Jim Lance for two years. His sister Claudia was his only assistant, and his mom Georgia was his front desk person. He was appreciative that I told him I might only be there for one year. He was wondering if having two assistants might make their days run more smoothly, so it was a permanent short-term agreement on both our parts.

Don was re-stationed a year later to Fort Lee, in Petersburg, Virginia—south of Richmond. In 1975, after fourteen years of marriage, we bought our first home in Chester, Virginia, halfway between his base and my job in Richmond. In 1976, I accepted a position with Dr. Richard S. Wilson, a general dentist who was opening his first office with zero patients. Helping Dr. Wilson build that practice from a start-up to a very successful operation in four years shaped my entire career in the business side of dentistry.

Across the highway from Dr. Wilson's new office, my friend Mary Ann worked for another dentist. Mary Ann had originally accepted the position with Dr. Wilson. He was a single dentist at age thirty-two, and Mary Ann was a divorcee for five years and was the same age. Mary Ann told me about Dr. Wilson, her new intended boss. She'd enjoyed meeting all of Dr. Wilson's dental school buddies that he'd introduced her to. The problem was, she had worked for the same dentist for ten years, and had a good salary and benefits that she would not have with a brand new practice with zero patients. She told me a couple of weeks after accepting the position that she most likely would not take the job after all. Dr. Wilson was going away for a week while his office cabinets were being built, and she planned to tell him upon his return.

I would *never* have divulged a friend's secret to anyone, but deep down I knew soon there might be an opportunity for me to possibly work for this new dentist if Mary Ann was sure she would not take the job offer. I called Dr. Wilson that evening to let him know that I was a friend of Mary Ann's and knew he had hired her, but wondered if he knew of any other dental assisting job openings on the south side. He did not, but said he would take my number and talk to some fellow Medical College of Virginia friends. A week later, he called to see if I had accepted another position. I had an interview with him that Thursday, and the rest is history.

Mary Ann had told him she could not leave the salary and benefits she had worked for ten years to have. Even though I took a $15 a week pay cut, I was happy to have found a job closer to home and with a wonderful thirty-two-year-old general dentist who had a fabulous personality, a great philosophy of patient care, and who was a great leader - before leadership was even a hot topic in business. That was 1976, the turning point in my career and the beginning of an employer/employee friendship that is still strong today—even though I have not worked for Dr. Wilson since 1980, when we moved to Virginia Beach with Don's last Air Force assignment. Dick and Ann Wilson are two of our best friends some forty-two years later. They are truly more like a brother and sister-in-law.

Lessons Learned as a Mom and Working Gal

Selling is serving. If you believe in your product or service, you can sell it.

Being alone seven and a half years out of Don's first fifteen years in the service created independence.

If you love what you do, you'll never work another day in your life.

Dentistry is a proud profession of changing smiles and changing lives.

Backward compliments are learning experiences that last a lifetime.

Success is a four-letter word, spelled W-O-R-K.

Chapter 9

The Foundation and Growth of My Consulting/Speaking Business

Dr. Wilson's office was small—about 750 square feet of space—and tucked away in the center of an L-shaped shopping center with barely any street exposure. When he opened the doors after a three-week delay due to construction, we were busy from day one, since he had been a full-time professor at Medical College of Virginia (now Virginia Commonwealth University School of Dentistry) after a four-year stint in the Army as a dentist in Germany. His patients loved him and referred their friends, family, neighbors, and coworkers. I was his only employee for the first eleven weeks until we hired Michie. Dr. Wilson told me when he hired me that I would be doing the front office *and* assisting until we got the practice going. He also told me that as his first employee, when we hired the second person, I could choose the job I wanted—administrative or clinical assistant.

While I loved assisting, he told me I had the personality to run his practice. But I knew by the first few weeks that it took more than personality to run a business. I asked if he would spend time training me on the business side of things, such as effective scheduling, confidence in asking for payments, overhead control, inventory, marketing, and budgeting.

He said, "I have no idea how all of that works...in dental school, they teach us to fix teeth, not how to run a business!"

I knew at that moment that unless one of us left and attended conferences on the business of dentistry, we were in trouble. I also knew that if he did not know about the business side of dentistry, there were about 160,000 other dentists who were in the same boat—so I assumed this *might* be my next business!

For the next year, I attended a few dental conferences, hoping there was a speaker on management and marketing. The more I learned, the more I knew I had to learn. Basically, practice management was in its infancy. There were no computers, no systems to speak of, and not many speakers on the subject. Ann Erlich was one of about three people teaching efficiency, verbal skills, or systems. She had great information that I loved, and I brought back her ideas and started creating "rinky dink" systems in three ring binders based on what I'd learned. I had a collections system for keeping track of past due payments and what patients said to me when I made collection calls. My 1-31 dividers (days in the month) indicated when to call the patients back if the promise-to-pay date was missed..

Then, I created the Pending Appointment System. Another three-ring binder held names, phone numbers, types of treatment, and units of chair time needed for that treatment. If the patient did not pre-schedule, this was how I kept track of pending treatment. When we had an opening in the schedule or a last-minute cancellation, I had names and contact information to quickly refill that open chair time. I also created an inventory control system to keep track of the minimum/maximum of supplies to keep on hand—where they were ordered, in what quantity, any back orders, and the price of last purchase. This saved money on over-ordering, running out of supplies, and not reordering back-ordered items. The rotation of the supplies in plastic bins on the shelves allowed me to take a bin off the shelf and restock the back, so the products did not expire. This kept our supply costs low, and we never ran out of clinical or business supplies.

Within one year, Dr. Wilson's dental school buddies started asking me questions in regard to our systems, marketing plans, etc. They who were across town in the white-collar section of Richmond—those who built very large showcase practices and were working five to five and a half days per week trying to make ends meet. They called to ask me if our practice was *really* doing the level of production per month that Dr. Wilson told them. He was still teaching at the dental school on Tuesdays, and only saw patients nine to eleven days per month. They were working twice as many days and producing only half of what our practice was producing.

When they asked about our numbers, I told them, "That is confidential practice information, but believe me, I have been in dentistry fourteen years and have never seen anything like our practice."

That's when they asked me what I did on Tuesdays while their friend, Dr. Wilson, was teaching. I told them that I was in the office every other Tuesday, working on my behind the scenes duties such as filing and following up on insurance, marketing projects, and doing collection calls. I was off every other Tuesday when Michie was there, doing her behind the scenes assisting work and covering the phones for me. They asked if I could come spend a half day per month in each of their four practices that were all twenty miles or so away.

Dr. Wilson gave me the green light, and that was how my consulting started. In 1978, I was in four practices a half day per month. From there, one of the dentists said, "We are now organized, and confident in our leadership and verbal skills. But more importantly than having an increase in production, we all *love* coming to work each day. Before you worked with us, we dreaded our confusion."

Another one of the four said, "You have so many great ideas that work—have you ever thought of doing a seminar and inviting lots of people?"

My response was, "Do you *really* think I can talk all day?"

He shook his head yes, and four months later, I held my first public seminar.

I spent four months writing what I felt was worthy to present, had a tacky brochure made, and did my first all-day seminar in March 1979, in Richmond. Thirty-six people came. From there, I did two cities each third month on my Friday/Saturday off in the same state. My next stops were Charlotte and Raleigh, North Carolina; Philadelphia and Pittsburgh, Pennsylvania; and Atlanta and Columbus, Georgia. I wasn't making much money, since my registration fees were very low—but it gave me practice! I was a terrible speaker back then! I made my first audio tapes in 1982, and shuddered when I listened to them years later. Thankfully, the speaker gets better—but the tapes don't!

After working in Dr. Wilson's practice for two years, Don was sent from Fort Lee, Virginia to Neah Bay,

Washington—on a Macaw Indian Reservation. The family could have gone for a two-year assignment, or I could keep my job, keep the children in their schools, and reduce Don's time to a fifteen-month assignment instead of two years. With a fifteen-year-old daughter and a twelve-year-old son, we decided as a couple that I should keep my job, keep the house another fifteen months, and not take the kids to this semi-remote assignment.

In the fall of 1979, I did a dental public seminar in Portland, Oregon and Seattle, Washington, so I could then go visit Don on the radar site for a couple of days. I hired a lady from church to stay with the children for five days. In Portland, when I checked into my hotel around 2 PM, the bellman told me that there was a seminar going on in the ballroom downstairs by two national speakers. I decided since it was raining and I had all afternoon/ evening I should go check it out. It was Mark Victor Hansen and Jim Tunney. Even though Mark was very well known some years later as the *Chicken Soup for the Soul* book series co-author along with Jack Canfield, he was virtually unknown at the time. Jim Tunney was then a National Football League referee and speaker. They spoke on leadership, etc., at a time when the topic was brand new.

When I travel on business, I wear business attire in case my luggage gets delayed or lost. That day I had on a navy-blue skirt suit with a dusty rose blouse and heels. I guessed, as I looked around the room, that I stuck out like a sore thumb; the audience was a group of lumberjacks. They were all wearing plaid shirts, boots, and jeans. The seminar was from 2 to 8 PM. We had an on-your-own dinner break from 5 to 6. I sat in the hotel restaurant alone at a table for two.

Mark, being the gregarious person that he is, ran over and squatted down beside me. "You're in our seminar, aren't you? Come and join the head table."

There were about ten people at the VIP table. I was thrilled to be sitting with the meeting planners, the speakers, and a few others who were friends of theirs. When Mark heard me say I was giving a dental management seminar the next day in the same hotel, he asked if I was a member of the National Speakers Association (NSA). I had never heard of them. He said that if I planned to make this my career, I should plan to be at the next annual convention in Chicago the following summer. Of course, I felt I could not afford to fly there and spend four nights in a big hotel on my very start-up fees—but Mark assured me that all serious speakers had to join NSA. It was truly the best advice that anyone could have given me, as NSA shaped my entire career as a speaker and taught me how to turn speaking into a business from a start-up hobby.

Dr. Wilson's office photo
Sherry Jones, Dr. Wilson, Linda (me)

Lessons Learned in My Foundational Years

A small dental practice can often be more profitable than a much larger one.

The business skills of dentistry are equally important as the clinical skills.

School is never out for the pro. Dentists and team members must continue to learn, continue to grow.

Without a mentor or guide to start a business, it's not easy.

When the student is ready, the teacher appears.

Chapter 10

Our Final Air Force Move

Within months of visiting Don at Neah Bay, Washington, he received orders for his last assignment with the Air Force: Oceana Naval Station in Virginia Beach for March 1980. We were happy with this news, as we'd enjoyed spending a few weekends visiting Virginia Beach the five years we'd lived in Richmond. LaDona was now headed into her senior year, and David was in the eighth grade. We were excited the orders were only two hours away in Virginia Beach, and even more excited to be a family once more.

I was ready to get my business of consulting and speaking off to a start, and did not plan to find a dental business job after relocating. But real estate in Virginia Beach was much more expensive than Chester, Virginia—the rural town between Richmond and Petersburg where we owned a home. In January, I went to Virginia Beach to meet with a realtor and look for a house. I had checked with a few dentists and dental friends in Virginia Beach to get recommendations of schools for the children. Don told me the most we could afford without my salary was a mortgage of $750, but the home I wanted in the best school district was close to twice that amount. Not only were the payments going to be $1,150 per month, but interest rates in 1980 were 21.5%!

I remember talking to the banker. With a very new part-time business, and Don's salary of less than $28,000 per year, there was no way we could qualify for the loan—even with a perfect credit rating. I took a temporary job—filling in for an office manager of a dental practice for three months while she was out for surgery—which qualified us for the loan. I could tell the banker was very reluctant, even though I told him I would work seventy or more hours per week in my business if he would just give me a break! Years later, after my name was in the local news for becoming an Inc. 500 company in 1987 and one of the fifteen finalists in the Hampton Roads Outstanding Professional Women in 1990, the same banker said he was sure glad he gave me the break I needed on qualifying for that home loan. We never missed a payment in 1980-82—during what we call our leanest years since Madera, California. But it was still a scary time.

In hindsight, moving in 1980 instead of 1981 wasn't the best idea, and our family went through some changes as well. Even though the kids had an option of the three of us staying in Richmond another year and having their dad commute two hours every Friday and Monday, they assured me that we should move right away. LaDona had only one more year of high school, and in retrospect, leaving her friends was not the best. Being a pretty new girl in her senior class, the girls who had been friends for years certainly did not accept her into their circles. The boys, of course, immediately liked her! That did not add to her popularity. She did not even have an interest in going to her senior prom. Growing up with those traditional things were the most important to me, but every generation is different.

We also moved from a rural, conservative area where school, work, church, and family were it. Moving to a beach and keg party town like Virginia Beach when our kids were teenagers with no close friends was not in their best interest—even though we all were anxious to be a family of four. In Chester schools, David had been interested in band, and played solo saxophone the first year in middle school. Then, in Virginia Beach, being in the school band was no longer cool, so he dropped out. Because Don and I were both in the high school band, his declined interest was a big disappointment. Side note: We actually named David after Mr. David Richardson— our band director who was a role model in our school years. While moving in 1980 later became a big regret for us, at the time we had no idea that it was not wise. As a military family, moves were a way of life.

When I tell new speakers and consultants today that it is tough to start a new business like mine, it reminds me of our first two years in Virginia Beach. I remember doing public seminars, which meant typing mailing labels, designing brochures, printing brochures, then paying the postage for mailing them. Snail mail was the only form of marketing back then, and remains the most expensive today. The whole family used to stick mailing labels on thousands of brochures while sitting on the den floor. We threw the brochures into mail bags, Don took them to the post office, and I crossed my fingers and prayed that the mailman would bring me enough checks to pay the printer so he could print more brochures!

There were many weeks of seventy to eighty hours of work, and no personal salary until the third year. Besides the monthly public seminars I booked and marketed, by late 1981 I was calling dental study club members and speaking two or three times per month in one-hour after-dinner lectures in eastern North Carolina. These after-dinner lectures were truly how I got busier. At the end of my after-dinner lectures, I mentioned that I had three Fridays open in the next ninety days for an all-day seminar for the dentists in the study club and their entire teams. Practice management and team training was very new in the early 80s, so I booked about nine out of ten of those I spoke for.

From the all-day lectures, I booked two to four in-office consultations. My consulting fees back in the early days were $1,800 for three days in office ($600 per day), which included twelve months of follow-up phone calls. At the end of my thirty-six years of consulting, my fees were $36,000 for the one year program. My early clients used to say, "We had Linda Miles when she was cheap!" I smiled and told them for as little as I knew back then compared to what I'd learned in three decades, my fees were most likely too high then and too low now!

Truly, management consultants learn from each assignment they are immersed in. And, as they learn, their content improves drastically—as well as their materials and the resources they share. After personally consulting more than 800 practices in thirty-six years, I truly could say, "I've seen everything." Consultants are like snowballs; you can't help but learn as you teach. We gathered more knowledge and value with each assignment, since no two practices were exactly alike. Also, as creative consultants, we established systems for each area of the practice—from collections and insurance management to inventory control, overhead control, scheduling, and reduction of failed appointments. We also covered case presentation, leadership, team meetings, and—most of all—positive communication skills.

In my opinion, it is impossible to speak and not consult or consult but not speak. The speaking brought the consulting assignments, and the consulting gave me tons of new speaking material. I never disclosed client names in lectures, and I changed the geographic area to protect the client identity. No matter what new practice management or "team wrinkle" I had solved months before in a client practice, rest assured there were dozens of practices in my next months' lectures that had the same or similar issues. They always appreciated the fact that they were not alone. And they appreciated the fact that I shared the solutions with them that day, versus some speakers who said, "And when you sign up for my XYZ Program, you will get the answer to that issue along with dozens more." Or, "If you buy my DVDs, all those answers are there."

I too developed products such as audio tapes, CDs, and DVDs—along with three practice management books. My first book, *Practice Dynamics (Building the Winning Team)*, was a Pennwell publication in 1983. My second book—with a short shelf life due to the changing insurance programs—was entitled *The Rise and Fall of Managed Care* (1993). My third book, which was self-published in 2003, was *Dynamic Dentistry*. If you are wishing to develop credibility, writing a book helps. With a publisher, you receive the standard 10% royalty with no guarantee of the number of books sold. Over seventeen years, my total income from book number one was less than $20,000. My second book was less income, as I only printed 1,000 copies—mostly for clients and seminar attendees. By self-publishing my third book and ordering 10,000 copies, I invested $65,000 over the span of a year. After meeting my breakeven point, the book brought in six figures and was a huge success.

Many speakers are fearful of creating products, thinking, *If I have products they will buy them, and not come and hear me.* Not true. So many dentists loaned my tapes or books to their colleagues, and we had calls frequently that said, "A friend loaned us your DVDs. When are you coming to XYZ city, as we want to bring our whole team to hear and meet you?" Even though I buy Michael Buble CDs, if he is ever in concert near us, Don and I always get tickets. Products are marketing tools and passive income centers. They enhance the speakers and consultants and help build their brand.

From the mid 80s to the late 90s, a seminar coordinator traveled to my lecture destinations—Sandy took over the West Coast and Virginia the East Coast. It was not unusual to be allowed the back of a room or a hallway table to sell products. Meetings have changed, and that is a rare happening today. Today, speakers must have sponsorship (dental companies that pay part of their speaking honorarium in exchange for promoting their products). I was retiring about the time things changed. With online webinars and downloadable materials, physical products are not the hot items they were twenty years ago.

One of the biggest nightmares of my early career happened in 1982 with a demo tape. At NSA, I heard that all speakers had to have a demo tape to send out to meeting planners. I had no idea how to go about making one, but I bought a small tape recorder. I decided, since my sixteen-year-old son's bedroom was above the kitchen and garage, that I would go upstairs to his room, arrange pillows on his bed as my audience, and make my demo tape. I called Don at the base and asked if the TDK tape I'd found in David's room was a good quality one. He assured me it would work well, so I proceeded to make the CD. We had fifty of them ordered and sent out about eight of them to meeting planners. My part-time assistant was coming to my house that day to work, so while making breakfast that morning I decided to listen to the tape. I usually did not listen to the contact information at the end, knowing what it said the last couple minutes.

That morning, the tape player was across the room on the table, and I didn't get to it by the end of the content. This is what it said: "If my team or I can be of assistance to you or your teams, please call this number_____." Then this horrible song came on. It was Jimmy Buffet singing,

"Why Don't We Get Drunk and Screw"! I could not believe my ears. Evidently, I had taped over David's song and hadn't even noticed! I quickly called my assistant to ask her how many of these had gone out. Then I played the last few minutes for her.

She quickly came to my house and started calling those to whom she had mailed tapes. She told them to discard the one we sent and a new one would be mailed that day. One dentist came to the phone and started laughing. He'd been in his office alone after work, paying some bills in his private office and listening to my tape. He heard the very ending and called his wife, saying, "Listen to this; something has gone awry in this lady's recording studio." Truly, if this didn't end my career, I guess nothing would have.

To this day, David (now fifty) says he has no idea whose tape that was in his drawer.

Lessons Learned in Our Move to Virginia Beach

Listening to our hearts instead of our heads by moving *before* LaDona graduated her last year was not a good decision, even though we thought it would be fine.

Going from a $384 monthly mortgage to $1,150 and quitting your full-time job in the same month is not a good idea.

The thousands you think will come to your first seminars might be dozens!

Consultants definitely learn something in every assignment they experience.

The dental speaking profession has changed dramatically in the past ten years. Sponsorship is king.

Many facets of dental management consulting are specialties such as HR, Insurance, Compliance, and Marketing.

Products are passive income—and if a speaker has a following, they can become a third of your business if marketed properly.

Don't ever randomly "borrow" one of your teenager's tapes to make your demo.

Chapter 11

My Secret Weapons

I credit my success to a supportive family and the hire of Lee Tarvin in February of 1984. I had other employees from 1981 to 1983 who did not pan out long-term. One of them stayed long enough to start her own business, another one hated living in Virginia Beach and came in daily with a bad attitude. Another was not organized and made two hotel reservations in the same city for me, forgetting she had made the first one. When I hired Lee, who had a background in dentistry, she was loyal and hardworking. She was also the most organized person I knew. After finding Lee through a mutual friend who had worked with her in a local dental practice, I refused to talk with her unless she had resigned her previous practice. I did not want to get the reputation of stealing employees from local dental offices. Lee sent me a copy of her resignation letter and we had lunch.

After she came onboard, it truly became a magical business. In 1988, along with two dynamite secretaries, Mary and Carol, Lee and I had to move out of the five-year leased building I'd rented in 1983. In 1987, Dental Dynamics, Inc. (trading as Linda Miles and Associates) was an Inc. 500 company with a 544% increase from 1983 to 1986. At our peak twelve years, when I was traveling about 200 days per year, we had ten on the corporate payroll and had six independent contractor consultants who had businesses of their own. A few of those were back-up consultants and speakers based on my busy schedule. These independent consultants paid the company a percentage of their consulting and speaking fees for the use of the name (Affiliate of LLM&A), their training, consulting, seminar materials, and my seminar leads. At our peak twelve years, we were a seven-figure business each year—not counting the gross production of the six affiliates.

In late 1997, I had lower disc back surgery at fifty-four and "right-sized" the business, not knowing if I would be able to continue at the pace I had been going. Looking back, I realize the back surgery was a blessing in disguise. My payroll during the final nonstop travel year was $333,000 for ten people in the corporate office, and my rent for a beautiful 3,500 square-foot office was close to $60,000 per year. I did a consultation of sorts on my own business. I came to realize I was working fourteen of those eighteen days per month to have a big office and lots of staff. By right-sizing—thanks to my daughter, who worked at the office at the time and found a much better location—the rent expense cut in half. We reduced the corporate team to four people, with two consultants for overflow. Over the next ten years until we sold the consulting, workshops, and products division in 2007, we built it back up to almost the same level of productivity with even more net profit each year.

Both of my children worked in the office for about six years each. LaDona was in sales and marketing, and with her dental hygiene background, she was great at keeping the consultants busy. David, with his art degree, was our graphic designer and copy editor. One day, he brought an article back to me and reminded me that a sentence could not have forty-two words. I reminded him that I wrote like I talked—a lot! David was not as dedicated to his job and the "rules" that all other employees adhered to, such as being on time for work. I reminded him several times that even though he was my son, I expected him to be on time. Many days when I was out of the office, he showed up late...but usually brought Starbucks and muffins to his coworkers as a bribe not to tell the boss! I've learned over the years that artists march to a different drum when it comes to work rules, but we loved the work he did.

Lee Tarvin was more than just a coworker, my Personal Assistant, and Chief Financial Officer of LLM&A; she was and still is more like my sister. Besides her kindness, her ability of remembering clients and meeting planners' names, exemplary organizational skills, and ability to lift her coworkers' spirits made my life less stressful and lifted many weights off my shoulders. Every person in business needs an "office wife," a person who looks after the details the boss doesn't need to be bothered with. Don ran the products division (a third of the business), and made sure all the tapes, books, etc. were shipped to the proper hotel or meeting site by the dates needed— and that the two men who worked in his department shipped all the orders for our DVDs and books.

Neither Don nor Lee would ever give me any stressful news or "wrinkles" on the home front or at the home office when I was on the road. They knew speakers must be "on" at every presentation, and not preoccupied with stressful things that someone else could take care of. They knew when I was in a client office, I was 100% with that office—which meant I wasn't trying to run my business or personal life while being paid to consult a paid client's business. We did not have cell phones or texting back then, but a ten-minute phone call during my lunch hour to check with Lee—for people I might need to contact between flights or at my hotel that evening—was the extent of my "off the clock" time with clients. If I taught dental team members to give 100% to their practice, I did the same.

It amazes me today how many dental team members use the Internet for non-dental business during office hours—and, worse than that, are constantly texting and making/taking personal calls during office hours. I once "fired" a client of three dentists when the two owner dentists and office administrator told me it was completely okay for all twenty-four of their employees (they needed fourteen) to use their cell phones during patient hours.

"We all have small children and elderly parents, and we don't want all our personal calls going through the front desk—so we have our phones on at all times for family calls," they explained.

This is the same practice that had listed time management as one of the things they hoped I could help them with. When I suggested placing all cell phones in lockers throughout the work day and met resistance, I knew *why* this practice ran forty to sixty minutes per patient late! I've only "fired" three clients in thirty-six years, and noncompliance big time was this issue. You can lead a horse to water, but that doesn't mean they will drink. Consultants/coaches are advisors, not magicians! We can't fix what the client messes up!

Over thirty-six years, consulting close to 1,000 practices from Tasmania, Australia to Toronto, Canada, I was privileged to work with some of the finest in dentistry. How wonderful when you get a Saturday morning phone call from a client of twenty plus years ago, who was visiting his dentist friend's lake house. They were reminiscing about their forty years in practice, discussing those who helped them the most along the way—and they decided to call me and say thanks! Or the dental spouse who lost her husband to sudden death. She took the time to call me after she received my card of sympathy and said, "I must tell you how many times over the years we toasted you for helping us have the lifestyle we enjoyed. And to also thank you for the rewarding patient and team experiences we had in our practice from following your teachings." Clients truly became lifelong friends in many of my consulting assignments.

So many of our clients remain my friends today, even though I—and many of them—have retired. The relationships I made during those years of travel made all the travel nightmares worthwhile. Some of my clients include: Dr. Jack Kayton, Dr. DeAnne Blazek, Dr. Jonathan Bregman, Dr. Tom McDougal, Dr. Ron Goldstein, Dr. Bob Randall, Dr. Bob Davis, Dr. Charlie Wood, Drs. Tim and Rose Clay, Drs. Greg and Lisa Mays, Dr. Greg Wych, Dr. Chris Cooley, Dr. Dave Lee, Dr. Denny Mills, Dr. Patrick Simone, Dr. Joel Safer, Dr. Louis Beall, Dr. Al Ousborne, Drs. Lisa and Casey Crafton, Dr. Jeff Landon, Dr. Ron Cavola, Drs. Darob and Richardson, Drs. David and Rebecca Swett, Dr. Kim Kitchen, Dr. Joel Hedgecoe, Dr. James Vollmer, and one of my later clients Dr. Tanya Brown. Tanya is my personal dentist and business partner in Ultimate Team Mastery. There were hundreds of others too numerous to mention, who were equally great and made consulting worthwhile. If they were all like these fine folks, I would have consulted until I was a hundred!

After thirty-six years of travel, at age sixty-three, it was time to look for a successor. I knew if I held onto the business I could net (in five years) the same amount I sold it for. But I also knew that I wanted someone to look after my client base after I fully retired, so selling it was the best option. After talking to a few competitors about merging my client base into theirs, the plan was that I'd keep on speaking a couple times per month, with all the consulting leads going to them. About that same time, a successful dentist client called Lee, asking her to have me call her.

When Dr. Rhonda Savage of Gig Harbor, Washington and I spoke, she said she wanted to buy my company. Rhonda was then forty-nine, about fourteen years my junior. She'd had shoulder surgery and had given up practicing clinical dentistry for about for years. She knew my material and had always wanted to be a speaker. When she'd asked me to consult her practice way back in the early 90s, my schedule hadn't had an opening for six months—so Char Sweeney, one of my top consultants since 1989, had visited Dr. Savage's practice in Tacoma. Rhonda had heard me many times at the Seattle King County Meeting, which I'd spoken at for about eleven years. She bought the consulting firm, two-day workshops, and products division in 2007. Rhonda became a busy speaker and consultant right away. She changed the company's name to Miles Global, which it remains today.

Lessons Learned as a Business Owner

In the speaking and consulting business, a big office with a large team is not wise. You don't have to be big to be successful. Keep it lean and clean (profit versus prestige).

Find out what's missing in any profession or business. Find a niche and fill it. For me, it was concentrating on the business side of dentistry. My focus was to create the best administrative teams in dentistry. Communication, Organized Systems, Motivation and the Art of Appreciation are the four principles I based my entire work on over the years. C-O-M-A...and that is what you have without those four basic skills.

Your body will tell you when it has met your "used by date" for constant travel.

Client and audience appreciation is the REAL paycheck.

Selling one's business is typically the start of that person's next phase of their life.

Retirement is not for everyone: "To Rest is to Rust." You must have other interests if you sell or retire.

The relationships created with clients, audiences, and colleagues are for life.

Chapter 12

Second Successful Business

In 1997, ten years before I sold LLM&A, many people wondered why I started the Speaking Consulting Network (SCN). After all, would these mentees not become my own competition, and competition for other established speakers? After individually mentoring eighteen colleagues in eighteen one-hour phone calls, telling many of them the same things, I decided to start SCN. Most of these mentees were folks I'd met in my audiences—those who loved what I did and wanted to also consult and speak. A few were dentists, but most were hygienists and office administrators who knew this was the next step on their career ladder. I decided to have a three-day conference in Orlando and create a how-to workbook of everything I had learned in the previous twenty years.

The workbook included check lists of what to do to hold and market public seminars; how to work with and get hired by meeting planners; my consulting model of assessment, interviewing, review of materials, and the all-day presentation (review of findings). It also included the how-to's of monthly monitors and client follow-up; marketing of consulting; retention of clients and a list of all the tools they need in their tool boxes. I included how to get published, then turn one article into a monthly column and eventually a blog or articles into a book. Eleven people came to the first SCN, with only one sponsoring partner (CareCredit). It grew over the next fourteen years to 150 in attendance. This included six meeting planners, four editors, and thirty representatives of leading dental companies as sponsoring partners.

Luckily for SCN, one of my all-time favorite mentees and a member of the SCN Executive Board for four years, Lois Banta—fifteen years my junior—bought SCN in 2010. It continues to grow and is truly the best dental networking opportunity if one is serious about starting or enhancing their own speaking, consulting, and writing businesses. There are so many superstars who have come back to SCN annually who are truly at the top of their game. It has been a joy to watch them grow year after year. They have now become coaches to the newer generation of speakers and consultants.

Some dental consulting speaking colleagues my age thought I was making a huge mistake training others how to start or enhance their own speaking and consulting businesses. These people came from a scarcity mentality that I was creating *our* competition. In fact, I was not sharing the pie and creating competition; I was simply making a much larger pie, as the founder of NSA Cavett Robert explained his NSA mission years before. A bigger pie represents more work for all of us. The abundance mentality is something I wish I could teach/instill in every dentist, company owner, consultant, or coach. The more professionals who share great ideas, the better each becomes. And what we pay forward or put into the Universe is exactly what we take away from the Universe.

I cannot tell you how my own business took off after starting SCN in 1997 and for the next fourteen years until I sold the Network. The more we share, the more we have coming back to us. My greatest joy is now sitting in the audiences of the next two generations of dental speakers, consultants, and coaches, and knowing that the basics I may have shared with them have created some pretty phenomenal people and businesses. The sixty-ish age group is entering the sunset of their careers and is truly at the top of their game; the fifty-ish group is clearly on their heels and will reach their prime within ten or fifteen years. The forty-ish group is still growing, and the thirty-ish group is the "newbie" who continues to amaze me with their spunk and confidence. They know that this business of ours is truly worth pursuing. They will be the next superstars in the next fifteen to twenty-five years.

Dr. Rhonda Savage had the first right of refusal to also buy the Speaking Consulting Network division. She declined that offer a few years into her own speaking and consulting, since she was super busy. In 2010, I was fortunate again with a second successor for that part of my business. I sold SCN to Lois Banta, a four-year member of the SCN Board and one of my SCN Executive Board members. My goal is to continue to support Rhonda and Lois, so that when they get ready to sell their businesses, they will be as fortunate as me in finding their ideal successors.

What does it take to succeed in this business? It takes creativity with one's material. You must have it on the shelf *before* you start to market yourself as the expert speaker, consultant, or coach.

You must have your marketing materials, such as: a website, speaker's one sheet or speaker package with a biography and professional headshot, short video, topics, titles, synopsis, and the objectives of each course.

It takes long hours and lots of travel. There are ways to create "passive income" through online programs, annual memberships, DVDs, podcasts, articles, blogs, books, and webinars. But before you create passive income, you must have a following who is willing to purchase your products.

Most of all, success only comes if you have a positive mindset. And you must have mentors to help you along the way. You must be organized and easy to work with in terms of follow-up and follow through with clients and meeting planners. You must always meet deadlines on reports, phone calls, emails, texts, speaker marketing materials, and articles. My advice is that every person in this business needs a PA (Personal Assistant) who does your travel, accounting, follow-up with meeting planners—and makes sure all deadlines are met. Understand that the creative side is important, but so is the detail side of things.

Lessons Learned in the Golden Years of Business

Death is the body's way of saying SLOW DOWN! Thankfully, my back went out before I died from traveling too much.

Finding a successor is not easy. They may know your material, but if they change the culture of the past years or decades too abruptly, the long-term clients/attendees will not be retained. While change is good, too much change at one time is worse than no change at all.

Sharing ideas and collaborating with others only makes each individual stronger and better.

You are your own competition. Better yourself each year and compete with yourself.

Chapter 13

Leaving a Legacy

One of my regrets in having lost my father in 1999 and my mother in 2004 is that they did not live to see me sell my businesses and slow down to the legacy part of my life. To me, these years are—in a different way—the most important. They are the give-back years. Selling one's business leaves a void, just as losing a parent or other loved one, so there is a transitional period of reshaping your days. I would not call this transition from working to semi or full retirement a form of mourning, but it is a loss all the same. This is why many of my dentist clients were saddened when they decided to retire . They did not have their next phase—Plan B—figured out. Golf and other hobbies are great, but they do not fill the void of practicing a career. Everyone needs to plan their legacy years. If their profession has been good to them, why not find a way to give back? Volunteering is the answer to fulfillment in the winters of our lives.

Don's mom came to live with us permanently in 2006, a year before I sold the consulting firm. She had lived with Jane, Don's cousin in West Virginia, for many years. Myrtle was a diehard West Virginian who wanted to live there the rest of her life. She was retired as a bank teller at seventy-six. She was active in the Bramwell Methodist church, and felt the annual making of homemade Easter eggs could not be done without her. But due to her failing health—and with more specialists in Virginia Beach than in Princeton/Bluefield, West Virginia—Myrtle had no choice but to make her home with us.

My children were now grown, and the grandgirls who I'd loved babysitting in the summers for a few years were now in college and almost grown, so it was a good six years of companionship. I can honestly say that even though Myrtle's mother (Granny Miles) had raised Don as her twelfth child while Myrtle worked away from the farm, Myrtle loved our two children and spent every birthday and Christmas with us as they grew up. She and I got along, but she had a very direct way with people— you always knew what was on her mind, and she believed in telling it like it was! We had a few disagreements over the years, and one *real* argument in the sixty years I knew her—the day she cleaned out the pantry and threw away all my spices since she felt they were aged! Try making lasagna with company coming that evening with no spices!

Even the times that she made me angry, I respected Myrtle; in those six years, she became my constant companion before her passing in 2012. We went to the dentist, her doctor appointments, shopping, the nail salon, the hairdresser—and a few times per year, she talked me into driving her to Dover, Delaware (four hours each way) to play the penny slots for two days. After Myrtle passed away from congestive heart failure and I sold the two businesses, it was time to embark on my new chapter from 2012 and beyond.

In 2007, Lee Tarvin's youngest son, David (age forty-two), was diagnosed with stage 4 cancer of the tonsil. His dentist found a spot on the back of his throat that was originally believed to be benign. Lee and I were at the Virginia Beach Resort and Conference Center doing a local two-day workshop the day of David Tarvin's outpatient surgery. During the surgery, they did a frozen section biopsy. Around 11 AM, Lee received a call of distress. The minor surgery they thought David was having was now turning into a very lengthy inpatient major surgery to remove the cancerous tonsil and lymph glands..

Shortly thereafter, our SCN Board met over dinner in Virginia Beach, and I explained to the board members that I wanted to start Oral Cancer Cause—to be able to financially help those head and neck cancer patients undergoing that type of extensive medical treatment. Besides being too busy to take on another project, I also did not know enough about nonprofits and developing a website at that time. So, I put this idea on hold for a few years.

In 2012, I met Robin Morrison at an AADOM (American Association of Dental Practice Managers) annual conference. Robin shared with me that she had recently lost her brother Mike (fifty-eight) to oral cancer. I shared with Robin that my sister-in-law, Charlotte (age seventy-two), was with hospice care—about to lose her battle of head and neck cancer at that moment. With Robin's marketing savvy and the research she had done when Mike was at his lowest point, it was a pivotal moment that we should become business partners and start OCC together. With her thirty plus years in dentistry and marketing savvy, and my fifty plus years in dentistry and knowing many, many people, we knew this was the combination needed to make this nonprofit successful.

I must say that our first few years were the hardest, but we also saw many highlights. At a nonprofit luncheon in Clearwater, Robin met an attorney from one of the major law firms that supports one nonprofit each year by providing all the legal work to set up the nonprofit pro bono. Robin submitted the forms, and we were the one they selected. What a blessing, which saved each of us about $5,000 in personal funds. We had our 501c3 status by 2013.

Being able to raise money for the families and patients of oral cancer has been a wonderful volunteer job in retirement. Robin, Amber Young, and I speak a half dozen times per year to raise money for OCC and many of the dental organizations like ADMC, SCN, and the Lucy Hobbs Project—and several other speakers and consultants have donated to the cause through their works. Amber Young, Executive Coordinator of OCC, along with our illustrious Board of Advisors have been a tremendous boost the past twelve months. We also have the greatest Ambassadors, who share our passion by spreading awareness. Our Champions are those who wish to hold events in their communities, making OCC the benefactor of funds raised.

The Oral Cancer Cause Bubble Challenge, Robin's wonderful idea, has been our single greatest project the past two years. This year (2017), we had three companies (Care Credit/Revenue Well/Benco Dental) as sponsors, and more than 300 dental practices all blew bubbles for those who can't.

Many communities sponsor Fun Runs or other community events for Oral Cancer Awareness. The big local event took place at UNIFY Health and Fitness in Virginia Beach in April 2017, in honor of Joe Cromwell and the four other survivors who attended. Interchrome Dental Lab and OCC co-sponsored the half day event. It was a huge success and had a good turnout. They had live music, food trucks, a bounce house, a fire truck, and face painting for the kids. The Virginia Dental Association offered free oral cancer screenings by volunteer dentists. The silent auction, donations, and raffle prizes raised more than $12,000. This event, along with the Bubble Challenge in April (Oral Cancer Awareness Month), raised more than $50,000.

In June 2016, Lee Tarvin and I—after working together for thirty-two years (since 1984)—decided that since we'd sold LLM&A in 2007, and also sold SCN in 2010, we must have been retired by now. We closed the corporation Dental Dynamics, Inc. (trading as Linda Miles and Associates) in June 2016. We also eliminated the P.O. Box mailing address, the office fax, and phone numbers. That *must* have meant we were fully retired! We would have more time to enjoy our family and friends, and do more traveling for fun.

Speaking of retirement—which I don't believe in, by the way—I watched my father retire from Kaiser Steel in California at age fifty-nine. Mom and Dad bought a small lake home in Lynchburg, Virginia to be near my brother Ted and his family and my youngest sister Bobbie and her family. Our sister, Pat, and her family lived in Richmond, and we were in Virginia Beach—for once all in the same state. Dad retired with no hobbies other than his airplane, which he kept tied down at New London Airport near Lynchburg. He flew it periodically, and liked hanging out with the airport folks. But due to too much food and TV, he literally atrophied his brain and body. Sitting in front of the TV watching CNN and snacking all day was not healthy.

Because Mom loved working at the post office as a postal clerk in Rustburg, VA, she kept working and later was a volunteer "pink lady" at one of the Lynchburg hospitals. Mom was truly a "people person"; she never met a stranger and loved doing things for others. Sadly, Mom developed a very rare neurological disease that mimics Parkinson's called Cortical Basal Degeneration—but the

Parkinson's medication doesn't help. My physician says it is so rare that no research has been done. The average lifespan after diagnosis is five to seven years (about how much longer Mom lived).

Because Dad had been a smoker for sixty years, he developed emphysema by age seventy-two. He could not walk to his mailbox and back, nor climb into his airplane anymore. Being the humorous man he was his entire life, Dad loved telling us that when he complained to his doctor that his right leg was bothering him, the doctor told him it was old age. He reminded the doctor that his left leg was exactly the same age and it was not hurting at all. After selling his Cessna, he truly lost his zest for doing anything. I think that is one of the reasons that I fear retirement completely. Dad passed away at age seventy-nine, and Mom followed five years later at age eighty-three. Losing our parents makes us face our own mortality. It means we are now the older generation and in the winter of our lives.

As long as I'm physically able to be active and continue staying involved in my many dental, church, and community-related interests, I will keep going. At seventy-four (by the time this book is in print), I feel great. I go to the gym three times per week and feel stronger now than I did at sixty-nine when I started working out regularly. I travel for fun with Don, the family, friends, and my two sisters, and totally enjoy a life of R&R. I feel blessed to have had the privilege to work with some of the finest dentists and teams in dentistry over thirty-six years. I enjoyed meeting audiences in all fifty states and on four continents. Some of my most memorable speaking engagements were the University of Zurich, the AAED (American Association of European Dentists) in Elsinore's Castle in Copenhagen, and the British Dental Association in Birmingham, England. I was also invited to the Barbados, Puerto Rica, Bermuda, and Bristish West Indies Associations. Five of my favorite highlights since

1992 were the five speaking tours I did in Australia for Port's Dental Laboratory and Power2B.

After visiting Australia and New Zealand in the early 90s, I met a wonderful Practice Administrator in Perth—Kathy Metaxas—who always wore a red jacket to my seminars. She stood out, and always came up to chat with me on breaks. She called me at home one day in November 1999 and said, "Remember me? I'm Kathy Metaxas from Perth, Western Australia! I'm close by and would like to come for a little visit."

"Red jacket?" I asked.

She was in America and wanted to know if she could come over for a few days. It was the day after Thanksgiving, and we had just received word that a favorite uncle (Don's cousin, Jane's dad) was in a serious condition and not expected to live. I had to go on assignment Tuesday, so Don had taken off to Charleston, West Virginia alone on that Friday. When I told Kathy that yes, she could visit for a few days and I was leaving Tuesday, she said she would be there the next day.

"Where are you?" I asked.

"San Diego, attending a Tony Robbins course."

"Well," I said, "you are 3,000 miles from Virginia Beach, but come over for three days."

Kathy and I became dear friends with lots in common—two children each, and love for dentistry and the people in dentistry. Her goal was to become the Linda Miles of Australia, and I was happy to help her get on the consulting and speaking track. She is now a superstar some eighteen years later. My meeting planner, Ruth Port, in Sydney, is also a dear Aussie friend. Instead of staying in hotels while Ruth sponsored me with Power2B seminars, I stayed at her home. Truly, these two women—who now know each other—are two of my best friends. We call ourselves the "Ya Ya Sisters." We have had so many friend adventures over the past two decades—I cherish the times we have gotten together on a cruise, in the Golden Door Spa in Australia, in Vegas, and in cities/beaches in Australia.

Don traveled with me extensively on speaking engagements, but not on consulting assignments. When you consult, you are truly "married" to the practice from the time you arrive until the flight takes off when your engagement is finished. After about fifteen years of traveling with me two or three times per month to various speaking engagements, Don took up golf as his hobby. He truly tired of the business travel before I did, telling me often when he ran our exhibit booth that his "smiler was broken." He enjoyed meeting my fellow speakers, consultants, and meeting planners, as well as the many friends/couples we met at the Hinman and meetings with the AADP (American Academy of Dental Practice).

In the past fifteen years, Don prefers to stay home and play golf while I meet up with my dozens of dental colleagues—who are also at dental meetings that I infrequently attend. It has become a real sisterhood over the years, with some of my very best friendships in those associations and conferences. Now that Don plays golf every day that ends in Y, it is difficult to get him away. I'd like to move to Sarasota, but he has his golf buds in Virginia Beach. I know that he can easily make new golf friends, since there are many golf courses in Florida. But I too love our retirement home in Indian River Plantation. Don has the lawn and gardens looking beautiful, and the back is truly a resort of its own.

In the past three years, I have developed an allergy to the mold in this region. After seeing many pulmonary specialists, my diagnosis is RAD (Reactive Airway Disease), which means that certain chemicals, mold, and pollen creates the on again, off again symptoms. I can be hoarse, sneezing, coughing, and wheezing, using inhalers—but within hours of being somewhere else, the symptoms disappear. Time will tell, since I don't enjoy masking my symptoms with medicine.

Fearing that I might get bored after retirement, I signed up at church for two committees, and joined a ladies' fellowship group that meets monthly and does other projects throughout the year. Like so many others who are retired, it is true that I don't know how I had time to work.

Lessons Learned in Volunteer Work

What you give, you get back in spades.

The harder I work, the luckier I become.

There are so many suffering from oral cancer. It devastates families, as well as the patient.

Retirement isn't healthy. As my friend Virginia Sullivan Stokes likes to say, "To Rest is to Rust."

What we put into the Universe is usually what we get back. Good deeds are like boomerangs.

Chapter 14

The Magic of Mentoring and Collaboration

In April 2016, I took Dr. Tanya Brown—my client since 2009 and my personal dentist since 2010—to lunch for her birthday. Tanya is a fantastic clinician, leader, and businesswoman. At forty-two, besides her phenomenal FFS (fee for service) practice and great team—which is a high-producing practice ten to eleven days per month—she is also a speaker and consultant on dental practice management. She told me at lunch a year ago that she had spoken in another state the previous Friday, and felt really bad because those dentists had wanted more of her time—but she did not have an opening for another six months! Her speaking and consulting works totally by word of mouth and fabulous results. I mentioned to her that some of my past clients had contacted me to help them by phone or Skype. They said, "You trained my administrative team twenty-five years ago; we have new staff, and I want you to work with us."

I explained to these former clients that I didn't do in-office consulting anymore, nor did I lecture at meetings. That's when I developed a two-hour tele-coaching program. Soon, I had about six dentists who also wanted the program. After doing it a few times, they started asking if I had more two-hour sessions. As one dentist said, "We need to be in touch with you four times per year."

I enjoyed reconnecting with these practices and loved hearing their successes by following my two hours of ideas. One program was Telephone Techniques; another was on Collections and Financial Presentations; and there was Case Presentations and Everyone's Role. The final one was on Marketing (Internally/Externally). Those programs went on from 2013 to 2016 when I had lunch with Tanya Brown. I explained to her that she needed to create two-hour programs that she could use to let each audience know that she had additional ways of connecting with them after she spoke at their meetings.

I went on to say to Tanya, "If I were tech-savvy—which I'm not—and if I had kept my CEU certification—which I didn't—I would offer two-hour live webinars every eight weeks for interval training. Interval training sticks better than 'fire hosing' the audience. I'd also invite lots of practices to join."

"Well, I'm tech-savvy and I have my CEU certification," she said with a grin. "Let's do them together!"

I had no idea that this would be the start of another business with another business partner. I told Tanya that by doing that, we could invite those who had contacted me or those I'd met since 2007 when I'd sold the company. She could use her database, and we could make this work.

Since I had closed my business in June of 2016, and had no desire to go back into business personally, Ultimate

Team Mastery (UTM) is part of Absolute Business Consultants (ABC)—Tanya's consulting firm. I am thrilled to be involved in her first series of UTM. We have given and recorded six two-hour sessions, with more than 200 people on each one. We did only social media marketing and made calls to our current lists. Tanya can take up to 1,500 people in the live sessions, but with our first sessions we kept it smaller by design. They are live at 11 AM EST on the first Thursday of every other month. In the fall of 2017, the first twelve fifty-minute topics are available online at a reduced fee of the live sessions. These twelve topics can be used for practices' one-hour per month in-house training sessions (team meetings).

With larger group practices today and the fact that dentists do not take their entire teams to dental meetings as they did in the 80s and 90s, online learning is huge. The feedback from the first UTM sessions has been extremely positive, with several practices reporting their best months ever this year. Others have said that *each* of the six sessions (two topics each time) had so many great pearls that each session is worth the fee we charge for the entire annual series.

Hearing the easy-to-implement information from a successful practitioner who uses the material in her own practice daily, and from a consultant with thirty-six years of experience, seems to be the "winning ticket"— according to those who have registered for the first series. Tanya and I have thoroughly enjoyed every work session and live session over the past year. I appreciate keeping in touch with dentistry and the people in it through UTM. The feedback we have had from those on the first UTM live series has made us extremely proud of the online program.

Going back to SCN annual conferences makes me even more excited about mentoring and collaboration, especially as I view those speakers and consultants I met more than twenty years ago who had just been starting to think about doing what they're doing now. I remember meeting Katherine Eitel and Janice Hurley, two young California consultants, at the ADMC meeting (Academy of Dental Management Consultants)—which started about nine years before SCN. My question to both of them was: "Why do I have to fly all the way from Virginia to speak at the California Dental Association meetings—an all-day trip going and returning—when the two of you are here?"

They both chimed in about the same time, "Oh, we are not speakers—we are consultants."

These two, in their early sixties, are at the prime of their speaking and consulting careers—and are two of the most sought after speakers in dentistry.

Lois Banta, a big follower of mine in Dental Association-sponsored seminars, called my office one day and asked me to hire her. I remembered Lois, because she was one of those people who had that magnetic personality you never forget. At five-feet tall and with a great big smile that matches her great big personality, my response to Lois was, "You don't want me to hire you—but I will help you start your own business." My son, David, created her first logo and edited her first article. Lois is ten-feet tall and bulletproof. I saw in her those traits necessary to do what I had been doing for twenty years. I could not be more proud of Lois and the fact that she is also my successor/owner of SCN some twelve years after her first conference.

The first day of SCN is for first-year members only. It is typically about twenty-five "newbies," as SCN lovingly calls first timers who attend. They could be experienced speakers/consultants/writers, or they could be like Lois—just staring their business. To SCN'ers, they are officially a newbie in the SCN family. On Lois's first day, she and about twenty others were asked to stand up on day one and introduce themselves to the audience. We wanted to know their name, location, number of years of speaking or consulting, how they heard of SCN, and their five-year goal. Many of them said they were Linda Miles followers.

When it was Lois' turn, she proudly said, "I am not a Linda Miles follower. I am a Linda Miles stalker."

I then asked her what part of dental management she enjoyed teaching the most. She thought for a moment and said, "I love going into an office and finding all the past due insurance money that is on the books but should be in the bank."

I told her that her tagline should be "Dentistry's #1 Dental Insurance Detective."

She truly made a huge name for herself early on with that moniker. Lois now lectures all over, on all facets of practice and team development.

Dr. Tanya Brown and Linda (me)

Lessons Learned in Mentoring and Collaboration

Magical collaborative ideas come forth from giving advice to a colleague.

Mentors learn as much—if not more—from mentees when they work on the same team.

Every time you teach, you learn.

Dynamite comes in little packages.

Successful people don't sit on the shore waiting for their ship to come in; they must swim out and meet it.

Setting goals is a great idea, but making promises to yourself is greater.

Lessons Learned
Throughout This Book

Growing up without money is actually a gift! Until we experience the lows, we cannot fully appreciate the highs.

While higher education is the best route to take, there are many people who for various reasons have not or will not earn a degree. Do I recommend they find a way to make college possible? Yes—but remember that with determination, hard work, and a learned skill, the American Dream is very much alive and well for those who wish to go a different, slower path to success.

Treating all people well, regardless of their social/ economic background, shows true character.

Clients and competitors can become your best friends— as long as both parties have the spirit of abundance.

Paying it forward is the way to go. It takes years to leave a legend. The foundation you set in your work years will determine your retirement legacy years. What is *your* legacy?

The more you give, the more you get! The Universe is good to those who give from the heart. Thankfully, I learned that from watching my mom in action.

No matter how successful anyone becomes, they should not—as Granny Miles used to say—"Get higher than their raising." In other words, stay true to your roots.

Starting a business is not easy. The reason so few make it is because they give up right before the magic starts happening. "Even a blind pig finds an ear of corn one day." 70% of the big ideas I had in thirty-six years failed miserably, wasting many dollars and many hours of time. But the 30% that worked, worked far better than I ever dreamed. It is those ideas that make you successful. Know when and what to fold if it is not working. Or back up, and take a different approach with the same idea.

Take care of your clients and team, and they will take care of you. Mentor those taking the same path you have been on. My coworkers were not my employees, but my shareholders—as Chuck Blakeman calls them. Many of my clients and dental colleagues became lifelong friends.

In building a business, learn to live on less than you could take from the business, and invest to the max. Then, your slow-down or semi-retirement years will allow you to live the life you deserve.

Above all else, find something you enjoy doing. Learn to love to do it, and then teach others to love to do it—not as *well*, but *better*!

About the Author

Linda Miles, CSP considers herself a forever learner. She is the founder of Linda Miles and Associates, an INC 500 dental management consulting company since 1978. She is also the founder of the Speaking Consulting Network, which has helped hundreds of other dental speakers and consultants start or enhance their own speaking/ consulting businesses. After selling her consulting business to Dr. Rhonda Savage in 2007 and the Speaking Consulting Network to Lois Banta in 2010, she started AskLindaMiles.com, an hourly tele-coaching business that requires no travel!

In 2012, she co-founded Oral Cancer Cause, Inc.—a 501 nonprofit that creates awareness of oral cancer and financially assists oral cancer patients during their diagnosis and medical treatment. Linda and her co-founder, Robin Morrison, founded OCC soon after Robin lost her brother Mike and Linda lost her only sister-in-law to oral cancer, both in 2012. After 50 plus years in dentistry, OCC practices and OCC's Advisory Board leave a legacy with many survivors in their oral cancer recovery process—which Linda considers her highest professional achievement.

After full retirement in 2016, Linda co-founded "Ultimate Team Mastery," an online interval practice management membership.

Linda makes it a point to stay abreast of changes in dentistry that will affect the next generation. She firmly believes that the fun and excitement of dentistry will never change for those who truly love it, enjoy their patients, and love working with their coworkers.

About the Work Linda Does

As a thirty-three-year-old dental auxiliary in 1976, I accepted a position in a small start up dental practice in Richmond, Virginia. Little did I know, being thrust into the business position of dentistry after fourteen years as a clinical assistant would completely change my life from employee to entrepreneur in a few years.

After helping train a few of my doctor's dental school buddies' administrative teams, I held my first public seminar in 1979. My topics were collections, telephone techniques, customer service, inventory control, scheduling, recall system, and marketing. I had developed these systems for my own dentist's practice, since back then there were no systems or computers. My little business would span over the next thirty-six years, and be an INC 500 company in 1987 for phenomenal growth.

In addition to starting Linda Miles and Associates with a team of ten in the corporate office and six speakers and consultants, I started a second business, the Speaking Consulting Network, in 1996. SCN held its first annual conference in 1997.

My consulting clients numbered more than 1000 practices with successful reports of highly skilled team members, satisfied patients, and happier, less-stressed dentists. We've held two-day workshops on the business of dentistry along with PAW (Practice Administrator Workshops) since 1993. About the same time, we started doing Sun Fun cruises for dentists and teams, along with "Ski and Learn" seminars and resort seminars, with hundreds in attendance.

In my mid-sixties (2007 and 2010), I sold both companies to devote more time to philanthropic work. Oral Cancer Cause (OCC) was founded in 2013 by Robin Morrison and me in memory of her brother, Mike Collins, and my sister-in-law, Charlotte Estep. Both lost their head and neck cancer battles in 2012. Robin and I met at a dental AADOM Annual Conference in 2012, and made OCC a reality after realizing our eighty plus combined years in dentistry and our passion to reach out financially to those families who are devastated by this disease. Our other mission is to create awareness that oral cancer does not discriminate. It is no longer a disease brought on by smoking and tobacco, as many in their twenties to forties who never smoked and rarely consumed alcohol are at high risk due to HPV. I also volunteer on two committees at Nimmo United Methodist Church in Virginia Beach. My "give-back" years have truly been the busiest and most gratifying of my life's work. I believe leaving a legacy should be everyone's goal.

Other Books by Linda Miles

Practice Dynamics, 1986, Pennwell Publishing Company.

Welcome to the dynamic world of dentistry—a useful, common-sense, and enthusiastic approach to managing a successful team and dental practice.

The Rise and Fall of Managed Care, 1997, self-published.

An open forum from seminar attendees and clients, with frank discussions of the conditions experienced by the general public and providers of health care when managed care becomes their reality.

Dynamic Dentistry, 2003, self-published.

Practice management tools and strategies for breakthrough success. A homerun for the transition of solo managerial style (by the owner) to the total team concept.

Co-author with Walter Hailey, Your Key to the Practice, 1995, Triamid Press.

A collaborative effort by two different, yet complementary, perspectives on how teams can be more effective. To help dental practices develop and own the twelve qualities most crucial for success.

Connect with the Author

Email:
lindamiles@cox.net

Phone:
(757) 619-1026

Address:
2788 Nestlebrook Trail, Virginia Beach, VA 23456

Websites:
www.AskLindaMiles.com
www.UltimateTeamMastery.com
www.OralCancerCause.org

Acknowledgements

This book would not have been possible without the people in my life who have woven the tapestry within these chapters.

To my teachers and neighbors who helped in my younger years; and to my elementary school friends, who thought I talked funny when I moved south, but eventually became many of my best friends.

I have such a deep appreciation for the National Speakers Association for creating the NSA that made my speaking business the success it became. I will cherish the CSP designation, the highest earned award for speaking excellence and many hours on the platform.

With deepest gratitude for the many dentists, teams, meeting planners, dental companies, and dental journals who believed in me early on and helped catapult my career. A special shout out to Dr. Howard Grant in Atlanta, who rescued my business when I almost cancelled one of my first public seminars due to low registrations. He not only came and brought his team, but called several of his study club friends and asked them to register. I am truly indebted to him! That one seminar was the start of something bigger and being asked to speak at Hinman, the largest meeting in the Southeast back in 1983.

A special tribute to my dear friend and meeting planner, Ruth Port of Sydney (Power2B). She invited me to do five speaking tours across Australia from 1992 to 2009. Australia became my favorite country outside the US. The people I met there, such as my other dear friend Kathy

Metaxas, made the twenty-four-hour flights and layovers worthwhile and fun.

Thanks to Dr. Jim Nelson, my first boss; Dr. Jim Lance; Dr. Steven Morrow; and especially Dr. Dick Wilson for hiring me, training me, and believing that there was life beyond the practice in the world of dental business.

A special thanks to all of my dental friends in the Speaking Consulting Network, the Academy of Dental Management Consultants, and those I worked with as co-workers in four practices. And, most of all, my corporate team and consultants, led by Lee Tarvin for thirty-two years. Without Lee's dedication and efficiency (she ran the business while I ran the roads), the success we enjoyed would *not* have happened.

Thank you to Robbin and the entire team at Crescendo Publishing for your support in helping me to finally write my story!

Thank you to Michael Barton, photographer from Princeton, West Virginia, for allowing me to use your beautiful picture on my book cover.

Last but not least, my parents Bud and Margaret Estep for giving me life. To my high school sweetheart and husband since 1961, Don Miles; our two beautiful children, LaDona and David; LaDona's two girls (our gorgeous granddaughters), Taylor and Jordan. Also, many thanks to our helpful son-in-law, Bobby, and our (bonus) beautiful granddaughter, Amy.

Even with your children grown when you start traveling, it's never easy to have your body on the road and your heart at home. But due to the love and support of our families that we speakers/consultants depend on, we are able to do our life work and share the rewards of all

LINDA MILES

those hours on stage by helping them fulfill their dreams. When people ask how Don and I stayed married all those years? It's easy. He traveled the first twenty-one years, and I traveled the last thirty-two—so we have had little time to annoy one another!

Linda (me) and David

119

Taylor, Amy, Bobby, Ladona and Jordan

Linda (me) & Don July 2010

Linda (me) & Don on cruise 2013

Don & Linda (me) Church photo 2016

Resources

1) NATIONAL SPEAKERS ASSOCIATION
   http://www.nsaspeaker.org/

2) SPEAKING CONSULTING NETWORK
   https://speakingconsultingnetwork.com

3) ORAL CANCER CAUSE
   https://oralcancercause.org

4) ULTIMATE TEAM MASTERY
   https://ultimateteammastery.com

5) ASK LINDA MILES
   www.AskLindaMiles.com

References

Armstrong, Thomas. 2012. "The Stages of Life According to Rudolf Steiner." *American Institute for Learning and Human Development (Online)*, August 7.

"Lifecycles." *Healthy, Happy, Holy Organization*. https://www.3ho.org/3ho-lifestyle/lifecycles

Life Script Doctor. 2015. "7 Chakra Life Cycles and Crisis Years." *Learning Mind*, May 7. https://www.learning-mind.com/7-chakra-life-cycles-and-crisis-years/

Sheehy, Gail. 1976. *Passages: Predictable Crises of Adult Life.* New York: E P Dutton.

Sheehy, Gail. 1996. *New Passages: Mapping Your Life Across Time.* New York: Ballantine Books.

Made in the USA
Lexington, KY
09 November 2017